Winning Shopping Center Designs

Winning Shopping Center Designs

28th International Design and Development Awards

 International Council of Shopping Centers

About the International Council of Shopping Centers

This book is based on the information submitted to the International Council of Shopping Centers 28th International Design and Development Awards program. Each shopping center featured in this book was the winner of a Design Award or a Certificate of Merit, as determined by the Awards Committee.

The International Council of Shopping Centers (ICSC) is the trade association of the shopping center industry. Serving the shopping center industry since 1957, ICSC is a not-for-profit organization with over 53,000 members in 98 countries worldwide.

ICSC members include shopping center

- owners
- developers
- managers
- marketing specialists
- leasing agents
- retailers
- researchers
- attorneys

- architects
- contractors
- consultants
- investors
- lenders and brokers
- academics
- public officials

ICSC holds more than 200 meetings a year throughout the world and provides a wide array of services and products for shopping center professionals, including deal-making events, conferences, educational programs, accreditation, awards, publications and research data.

For more information about ICSC, contact:
International Council of Shopping Centers
1221 Avenue of the Americas, 41st Floor
New York, NY 10020-1099
www.icsc.org

This publication is designed to provide accurate and authoritative information in regard to the subject matter covered. It is sold with the understanding that the publisher is not engaged in rendering legal, accounting, or other professional services. If legal advice or other expert assistance is required, the services of a competent professional person should be sought.

> *—From a Declaration of Principles jointly adopted by a Committee of the American Bar Association and a Committee of Publishers.*

Companies, professional groups, clubs and other organizations may qualify for special terms when ordering quantities of more than 20 of this title.

Published by
INTERNATIONAL COUNCIL OF SHOPPING CENTERS
Publications Department
1221 Avenue of the Americas
New York, NY 10020-1099

BOOK DESIGN: Harish Patel Design, New York, NY

ICSC Catalog Number: 258

International Standard Book Number: 1-58268-052-3

Contents

About the ICSC International Design and Development Awards

The ICSC International Design and Development Awards Program was established to recognize outstanding shopping center projects and to provide information on them to the entire industry so that others may benefit from the experiences of their colleagues.

The 28th International Design and Development Awards Program was worldwide in scope. Participation in other ICSC design awards programs, such as the Canadian or European awards, did not preclude eligible projects from being considered for an International Design and Development Award.

Projects that opened within the 24-month period from July 1, 2001, to June 30, 2003, were eligible for entry into this year's Awards Program.

Awards Categories

Categories for entries were:

Category A—Renovation or Expansion of an Existing Project
Entries had to relate to a project involving an entire shopping center, such as an enclosure, or a single facet of a center, such as an addition. The renovation or expansion must have been completed and the center fully opened for business within the 24-month period from July 1, 2001, to June 30, 2003. Eligible subject matter included, but was not limited to, improving the use of existing space, methods of keeping a center open during construction, new marketing and re-leasing approaches, refinancing techniques, innovative design and construction approaches, and adaptive reuse of the structure.

Category B—Innovative Design and Construction of a New Project
Entries had to relate to a specific new shopping center, completed and opened within the 24-month period from July 1, 2001, to June 30, 2003, and must have demonstrated how a specific design or construction problem was solved or how new standards in design or construction were established. New methods of environmental enhancement, space utilization design themes, energy conservation and innovative construction techniques were among the subjects that were considered for this category. Entries included

detailed information about the design and construction of the center, such as explanations of the reasons for, and the realized accomplishments of, the particular approach.

Awards Classifications

Entries submitted for either **category** were judged according to the following center **classification** system:

1. Projects under 150,000 square feet of total retail space*

2. Projects of 150,001 to 500,000 square feet of total retail space*

3. Projects over 500,001 square feet of total retail space.*

*Total retail space includes all square footage included in gross leasable areas (GLA), all department store or other anchor square footage, movie theaters, ice skating rinks, entertainment centers and all peripheral (out-lot) space engaged in retail enterprise. It does not include office or hotel square footage.

Eligibility

1. The ICSC International Design and Development Awards Program was open only to ICSC member companies. Any ICSC member company could enter as many projects as desired in either of the two categories.

2. Entries must have had the authorization and signature of the owner or management company of the property.

3. Projects opened within the 24-month period from July 1, 2001, to June 30, 2003, were eligible.

4. Projects must have been completed and opened for business by June 30, 2003.

5. Separate phases of a project could be submitted individually, provided they were completed and opened for business by June 30, 2003.

6. Projects could only be submitted once. Projects that were entered in the past could not be resubmitted unless substantial changes were made since the last submission.

7. Members entering the ICSC Canadian or ICSC European awards programs had to submit separately to the International Design and Development Awards Program, and entries had to adhere to its entry guidelines and requirements. Entries accepted into other ICSC awards programs did not automatically qualify for this program, nor was any entry excluded simply because it was an award winner in another program.

If you have any questions about the International Council of Shopping Centers International Design and Development Awards, or would like to receive an application for the upcoming awards program, please contact:

International Council of Shopping Centers International Design and Development Awards 1221 Avenue of the Americas 41st Floor New York, NY 10020-1099 (646) 728-3462 www.icsc.org

Foreword

This year's entries to the 28th ICSC International Design and Development Awards Program were truly international. There were 50 entries from 15 U.S. states and 15 other countries – from Florida to California, from Australia to Korea and Japan, from the Netherlands to Poland and Germany, from France to Portugal and Turkey, and from Canada to Brazil and Ecuador.

There were 11 finalists in the Category of *"Renovation or Expansion of an Existing Project."* Many had been retail successes for 40 to 50 years, such as Canberra Centre in Australia, Dadeland Mall in Florida and Le Carrefour Laval in Canada. Others were mixed-use complexes, such as the Prudential Center in Massachusetts. Owners, developers, designers and contractors found ways to update the old models into modern, attractive retail formats. In doing so, they have added another 30-plus years to the life of these centers.

There were 28 finalists in the category of *"Innovative Design and Construction of a New Project."* New levels of creativity abounded in projects small and large. Hoshigaoka Terrace in Japan is a 141,000-square-foot open-air center on a sloping site. Madrid Xanadu in Spain incorporated a 245,000-square-foot Snow Dome into the 1.7-million-square-foot project. The Mall at Millenia in Orlando, Florida, combined restaurants on a streetscape with an upscale tenant mix in a leading-edge internal art form that included computerized water features and huge video screens on the central court choreographed to music.

For almost three decades, the worldwide recognition of outstanding projects has formed the basis of the ICSC International Design and Development Awards Program. The historic standards of excellence were reflected this year in the nine Design Award winners and the 15 Certificate of Merit recipients.

The International Design and Development Awards Jury Committee is composed of 11 industry leaders from development, retailing, architecture, construction management, financial investment and consulting firms. They average 25 years' experience and invest many hours in judging submissions and improving the professional quality of the program. I am very grateful to them for their dedication and professionalism.

For the past several years, the Awards Committee has worked to enhance the international nature of the program and to increase the recognition of owners, developers, architects, retailers, designers, cities and contractors for their creativity, resourcefulness and hard work. For the first time, we announced the International Design and Development Awards winners at the December 2004 ICSC CenterBuild Conference in a special awards ceremony. We will continue to feature the winning projects at the annual ICSC Spring Convention, as we increase the professional recognition of the International Design and Development Awards program.

As I complete my seventh year as Chairman and 17 years on the Jury Committee, I thank the ICSC membership for the honor of serving you in this exciting professional program. I hope this book of winning entries inspires future projects that will provide world-class shopping and entertainment experiences.

Daryl K. Mangan
Birmingham, Alabama

Chairman
ICSC 2004 International Design and Development Awards
Jury Committee

Acknowledgments

The International Council of Shopping Centers 28th International Design and Development Awards were selected by a committee of diverse shopping center professionals representing retailers, developers and architects. The International Council of Shopping Centers is grateful to these judges for the time, effort and expertise they contributed to the awards program.

Daryl K. Mangan, *Chairman*
Birmingham, Alabama

Ronald A. Altoon, FAIA
Altoon + Porter Architects
Los Angeles, California

Tom Brudzinski
The Rouse Company
Columbia, Maryland

F. Carl Dieterle, Jr.
Simon Property Group
Indianapolis, Indiana

Arcadio Gil Pujol, ASM
LaSBA, S.A.
Madrid, Spain

Gordon T. Greeby
The Greeby Companies, Inc.
Lake Bluff, Illinois

John M. Millar, SCSM
Divaris Real Estate, Inc.
Virginia Beach, Virginia

J. Thomas Porter
Thompson, Ventulett, Stainback & Associates
Atlanta, Georgia

Rao K. Sunku
J.C. Penney Co., Inc.
Dallas, Texas

Ian F. Thomas
Thomas Consultants, Inc.
Vancouver, BC, Canada

Gerald M. White
Copaken, White & Blitt
Leawood, Kansas

Almada Forum

Almada, Portugal

Owner:

Commerz Grundbesitz Investmentgesellschaft mbH
Wiesbaden, Germany
and
Group Auchan
Lisbon, Portugal

Development Company:
AM Development
Lisbon, Portugal

Design Architect:
T+T Design
MC Gouda, The Netherlands

Production Architect:
Beeking en Molenaar Den Haag, B. V.
Lisbon, Portugal

Graphic Design:
Novo Design
Lisbon, Portugal

Lighting Designer:
Har Hollands
Lisbon, Portugal

Landscape Architect:
Broadway Malyan
Lisbon, Portugal

General Contractor:
CPH – Companhia Portuguesa de Hipermercados, S. A.
Lisbon, Portugal

Development and Leasing Company:
AM Development
Lisbon, Portugal

Gross size of center:
74,500 sq. ft.

Type of center:
Regional center

Physical description:
Enclosed three-level mall

Location of trading area:
Suburban

Population:
- Primary trading area
  315,000

- Secondary trading area
  342,000

- Annualized percentage of shoppers
  anticipated to be from outside trade area
  25%

Development schedule:
- Original opening date
  September 18, 2002

Parking spaces:
- Present number
  5,000

*A*lmada Forum is designed as both a retail venue and a modern-day meeting point for residents of suburban Lisbon. The mall, located at the intersection of two major highways and a bridge leading to a populated peninsula, also attracts tourists, who comprise about one-fourth of its shoppers.

Each area of the mall has a distinct ambience. A Village Square at the main entrance is the site of community functions and exhibi-

The main entrance (left) and a sign (above) introduce shoppers to Almada Forum in suburban Lisbon.

tions. It also commands a fine view of the city and the famed Cristo Rei monument. Tree-like columns with conical skylights and a "floating" roof enhance the impression of an open forum. Panoramic escalators carry visitors from the parking level to the second-floor food court and cinemas.

The Village Square plaza also introduces shoppers to the array of artwork in the mall. At the entry, glass-encrusted mermaid statues by the Dutch artist Carla include one that is over 20-feet high. Outside, Dutch artist William Rutgers shows weather vanes in the form of fish.

Another area is the Experience Nature Atrium, whose theme is the earth and the sun, and which features a naturally lit large glass dome supported by arching wood columns. In the dome, a suspended mobile with a school of fish continues the nature theme. A large sculpted rock spans several

An aerial view (far left) shows the nature dome at the center. The high-tech roof of the Education Center (right) suggests a Byzantine temple. A glass-encrusted mermaid's face (opposite page, below) and a dramatic entry (below) show a high priority for striking design.

MAJOR TENANTS		
NAME	TYPE	GLA (SQ. FT.)
Hypermarket Jumbo	——	129,167
Warner Lusomundo cinemas	Multiscreen Theater	60,386
Fnac	Leisure	26,899
Zara	Apparel	23,895
C&A	Apparel	23,724
Toys"R"Us	Toys and Apparel	23,013
Sportzone	——	12,518
Cortefiel	Apparel	10,903
Macmoda	Apparel	8,966
Chimarrão	——	8,902

Design is everywhere at Almada Forum. Even artwork drawn from nature is given multiple interpretations, including a foam-like giant cactus and etched plate glass overlooking a court.

Effective use of natural light unifies the three-story mall format.

stories and contains lush vegetation and a waterfall; the rock was designed by the Catalan artist Javier Barba. Special lighting effects elsewhere in the atrium include a volcano-like image.

Shoppers explore technological themes in the Education Court, dominated by geometrical and high-tech design. The court's roof is shaped somewhat like a Byzantine temple and creates a darker and self-contained space, which in turn is punctured by spiraling skylights illuminating the shopping court below. Keeping with the concept, the storefronts here show modern design in glass and steel.

The main thoroughfares of the mall are the Lunar and Solar Avenues. There are seating areas, large overhead skylights and sculptures. The design uses natural materials — timber bridges to connect upper levels and facades of stone and brick. Shopfronts feature bay windows and balconied arcades. Indigenous flora and

fauna are used throughout, reflecting the Portuguese tradition of rich landscaping.

The third level holds the 35-shop, 1,200-seat Bay View Food Court. Its name is based on a familiar-sounding but nonetheless fictitious city. The design links the area to the region's cultural background and its nautical and maritime history. The "floating" roof has an oyster-shaped skylight. Restaurant facades remind shoppers of a traditional seaport. Some seating areas have outside terraces. The Coral Gardens section offers views of the Experience Nature Atrium.

Vegetation (left) is brought indoors but does not block views of shopping destinations at all levels.

Classically inspired murals (above), stone and tiled seating areas (right) and an outsized cinema (below) all blend in a varied setting at Almada Forum.

A theme tent structure on the roof is the site of children's activities. The third-level Warner Lusomundo cinemas seats up to 3,800 patrons at 14 screens. A bowling alley is adjacent to the cinemas.

Almada Forum has 260 small shops on its three floors, in addition to its hypermarket and cinema anchors. Two parking levels provide 5,000 vehicle spaces. A separate exterior area provides parking for staff. Construction on the center started in July 1999 but stopped eight months later because of licensing problems. Work resumed in September 2000 and lasted another 24 months. The site includes a road network.

Community gathering place and art gallery — and a design ranging from the natural to the technological — all at Almada Forum.

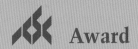

Ayala Center Greenbelt 3

Makati City, Philippines

Owner:
Ayala Land, Inc. (ALI)
Makati City, Philippines

Management Company:
ALI Commercial Centers Group
Makati City, Philippines

Design Architect:
Callison Architecture, Inc.
Seattle, Washington, United States

Production Architect:
GF Partners
Makati City, Philippines

Graphic and Lighting Design:
Callison
Seattle, Washington, United States

Landscape Architect:
Edward D. Stone & Associates
Santa Monica, California, United States

General Contractor:
Makati Development Corporation
Makati City, Philippines

Development Company:
Ayala Land, Inc. (ALI)
Makati City, Philippines

Leasing Company:
ALI Commercial Centers Group
Makati City, Philippines

Gross size of center:
300,000 sq. ft.

**Gross leasable area
(small shop space, excluding anchors):**
218,224 sq. ft.

Total acreage of site:
6.4 acres

Type of center:
Lifestyle center

Physical description:
Open mall

Location of trading area:
Urban but not Central Business District

Population:
• Primary trading area
  4.5 million

• Secondary trading area
  approximately 5.4 million

• Annualized percentage of shoppers
  anticipated to be from outside trade area
  33%

Development schedule:
• Original opening date
  December 2002

Parking spaces:
• Present number
  838

*Cinemas (right)
are an anchor in
Greenbelt 3, a
retail and leisure
destination in
Makati City,
Philippines.*

*G*reenbelt 3 — a dining, entertainment and shopping destination — is a four-story open-air pavilion in a park. It is located within Ayala Center, a mixed-use complex in the central business district of Manila, the Philippines. Greenbelt 3 is connected to other commercial buildings by an elevated walkway that also links to Makati's network of elevated pedestrian thoroughfares.

Given the harsh Philippines environment of heat, humidity and strong rains, most malls in the region rely on an air-conditioned "box" for a retail setting. Greenbelt 3, however, has an indoor-outdoor ambience with a design that alleviates the climatic burdens. Louvers and canopies aid ventilation and offer protection

MAJOR TENANTS		
NAME	**TYPE**	**GLA (SQ. FT.)**
Cinemas	Multiscreen theater	28,410
Food Choices	Café	20,016
SSI	——	15,732

The design of Greenbelt 3 (far right) fits in with the tones of its native surroundings. Sloping metal roofs (below right) cool the center from the harsh Philippines heat.

From a restaurant balcony (below), shoppers can view the adjacent park and downtown.

from the rains. Sloping metal roof planes with generous overhangs give additional shade and shelter.

The project essentially fit in around existing features, including the park, a church and a museum. The developer also sought to keep all the trees on the site as well. Knowing that retailers desire street locations with high traffic and that residents love the rare park spaces in town, a garden-wall concept was created to offer both urban and natural surroundings. The city side of the project presents a unified front and the street presence required by businesses. The park side of the project virtually grows into the terraced building, which weaves through meandering courtyards and pathways that also

give outdoor seating for cafés and restaurants.

The developers saved nearly 440 trees during the development process, including lush groves of mature acacia, palm and banyan trees. Another 200 trees, shrubs, flowering plants and water features were added to the park, whose acreage was nearly doubled. The area originally set aside for the park could have accommodated one more building — and more revenue — but the developer thought that "greening" the project was a higher priority.

Throughout the project, local design references abound. The wood tones used in the elevated walkway fit with surrounding natural materials. Water features are visible in every direction. The bases of the many saved trees are clad in stone planters. Grassy areas adjoin the flowerbeds passed by shoppers on their way to stores.

Stores are located in a series of four-story pavilions, carefully placed to respect existing land uses. "Quiet" tenants, such as a bookstore and galleries, were placed next to the existing museum at the project's north end. Next are tenants focused on home and apparel, sited with the restaurants near an active intersection. Finally, farthest from the museum, is a lively zone containing music and video stores, more dining, the cinemas and nightlife destinations.

Water features, lush vegetation, canopies and open ventilation make the indoor-outdoor ambience work.

More than 80,000 people visit Greenbelt 3 each day, providing continuous shopper traffic well into the night for the Philippines' first lifestyle center.

Part park, part shopping center (left), Greenbelt 3 provides an oasis in downtown. Smart design and plenty of shade (right) make air-conditioning irrelevant at Greenbelt 3.

Birkdale Village

Huntersville, North Carolina, United States

Owner:
The Inland Real Estate Group, Inc.
Oak Brook, Illinois, United States

Residential Management:
Crosland, Inc.
Charlotte, North Carolina, United States

Retail Management and Marketing/Events:
Pappas Properties, LLC
Charlotte, North Carolina, United States

Master Planning and Conceptual Design:
Shook Kelley, Inc.
Charlotte, North Carolina, United States

Co-Architects of Record:
Shook Kelley, Inc.
Charlotte, North Carolina, United States
and
The Housing Studio
Charlotte, North Carolina, United States

Landscape Architect:
LandDesign
Charlotte, North Carolina, United States

Leasing Company:
Crosland, Inc.
Charlotte, North Carolina, United States

Gross size of center:
725,185 sq. ft.
(including 54,157 sq. ft. of office space and
382,047 sq. ft. of apartment space)

Gross leasable area:
288, 981 sq. ft. of retail space, including
53,200 sq. ft. of theater space

Total acreage of site:
52 acres

Type of center:
Neighborhood/community lifestyle center

Physical description:
Open mall

Center's trade area:
Suburban

Population:
* Primary trading area
  36,929

* Secondary trading area
  46,887

* Annualized percentage of shoppers
  anticipated to be from outside trade area
  12%

Development schedule:
* Original opening date
  September 2002

Parking spaces
* Present number
  2,101

Photographs: Patrick Schneider

*B*irkdale Village in Huntersville, North Carolina, is a 52-acre mixed-use planned community incorporating office, retail and residential. It offers a pedestrian-oriented urban environment that is both an oft-visited regional destination and a home for hundreds of residents.

Because the three uses are mostly stacked above one another, timing of development was a major issue. For example, if the upper-level residential units were to be ready for a spring/summer opening, construction had to begin on the ground-floor retail level before leasing was completed. Later, residential would be occupied while retail was upfitted below. Several steps eased this situation. The concrete depth of the floor separating the retail from residential was increased beyond code requirements. A series of empty shafts were installed to provide

Reminiscent of an earlier era, Birkdale Village is a mixed-use community with retail, office and residential uses.

Birkdale Village

- ■ Upper Floors Office Space/ Lower Floors Retail
- ■ Residential Space only
- □ Outparcels
- ■ Cinema
- ■ Restaurant only

future flexibility for retailers' vents and plumbing lines. Road improvements were managed to have minimal impact on residential traffic flow. Finally, a soft economy enabled the doubling of the size of the construction crew.

Despite complications, opportunities evolved during construction as well. Midway through Phase I, a noteworthy number of national retailers became interested in the project. Phase II, which was to

have been entirely residential, instead incorporated more retail space to satisfy the national chain stores.

A number of managerial steps facilitated construction. With multiple owners pushing agendas appropriate to their particular uses, ongoing conversations were essential, so all parties met each Tuesday for the length of the project. Accountants and financial professionals used only one over-

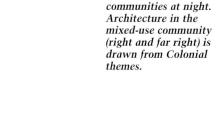

Lively street scenes (above) are rare in North Carolina communities at night. Architecture in the mixed-use community (right and far right) is drawn from Colonial themes.

Evident in the rendering (top) and the aerial view later (left), the mall section is closest to the major highway.

all project budget, carrying a single pro forma for the entire project. Since building codes for mixed-use projects are undefined — and may vary from building to building — the developers initiated early communication with local code officials and maintained a dialogue with supervisors to make sure nothing was lost during the transition of city personnel.

Planning also focused on user needs on such matters as parking. Residents want to park close to their front door. Retail tenants need customer parking, loading zones and back-of-shop areas. In the project, the bottom floor is public parking, placing retail patrons directly behind the shops.

Birkdale Village (top) offers on-street parking, retail at street level and residences above. A family outing (above) recalls the days of thriving downtowns.

Varied exterior finishes on the upper residential floors show that planned communities need not look "planned."

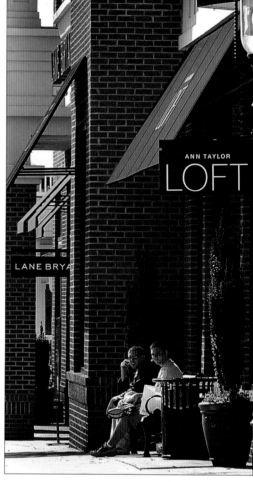

An exciting mix of national retailers coexists with traditional design touches.

MAJOR TENANTS

NAME	TYPE	GLA (SQ. FT.)
Eastern Federal Theater	Multiscreen stadium cinema	53,270
Dick's Sporting Goods	Sports	32,010
Barnes & Noble Booksellers	Bookstore	23,000

The "BV" logo (left and above) adorns signage and plant grates. The mid-street row of tulips, however, needs no adornment.

The upper parking floor is keyed-entry only, allowing residents to walk from their cars to their front doors on the second floor.

Good planning relieved many potential stressors between residents and retailers. Residential move-ins were limited to certain hours and days to avoid blocking retail operations. To minimize noise, retail loading alleys were built below parking decks, out of residential view. Compactors have ozone and odor containment and are located below the parking decks, close to retail shops — they are not below residential bedroom windows, nor are they visible from above.

The mix is working. The first Fourth of July celebration drew 500 attendees, though three-fourths of the shops had not yet opened. Nearly 5,000 people attended the annual Christmas tree lighting. Birkdale Village teamed with Habitat for Humanity to build Santa's cabin, where kids could have photos taken — the campaign raised $12,000 for Habitat and a subsequent auction of the cabin netted $20,000 more for the charity. From its earliest days, Birkdale Village was recognized as the center of a new community by retailers and residents alike.

El Muelle Leisure and Shopping Centre

Las Palmas de Gran Canaria
Las Palmas, Spain

Owner:
Riofisa, S. A.
Alcobendas, Madrid, Spain

Management Company:
Knight Frank
Madrid, Spain

Design Architect:
Riofisa — Chapman Taylor
Alcobendas, Madrid, Spain

Production Architect:
Idom
Madrid, Spain

Graphic Design:
Chapman Taylor
Madrid, Spain

Lighting Designer:
International Lighting Consultants (Theo Kondos)
New York, New York, United States

Landscape Architects:
Arceval Jardinería
Madrid, Spain

General Contractor:
OHL
Madrid, Spain

Development Company:
Riofisa, S. A
Alcobendas, Madrid, Spain

Leasing Company:
Knight Frank
Madrid, Spain

Gross size of center:
682,571 sq. ft.

**Gross leasable area
(small shop space, excluding anchors):**
367,027 sq. ft.

Total acreage of site:
1,557 acres

Type of center:
Community/regional fashion/specialty center

Physical description:
Enclosed five-level (retail) mall

Center's trade area:
Urban Central Business District

Population:
• Primary trading area
355,563

• Secondary trading area
482,253

• Annualized percentage of shoppers anticipated to be from outside trade area
9%

Development schedule:
• Original opening date
April 11, 2003

Parking spaces:
• Present number
1,300

Exterior materials used at El Muelle in the Canary Islands had to have high resistance to marine abrasion.

*E*l Muelle, in Las Palmas in Spain's Canary Islands, is an urban center designed for commercial and entertainment uses. It is located in the city center, next to the bus station and inter-island ferry terminal. Reflecting its island setting, the center's structure is modeled like a ship anchored in port, with stepped terraces that minimize its impact on the seafront. At one point, the building is less than 15 feet from the Atlantic Ocean.

The center contains seven levels, two for parking and five for retail and entertainment — a configuration that proved challenging to the development and design team. The island location causes the water table to be very near the surface. The small site required multilevel parking. With the high

water table, only one of the parking lots could be partially underground; the other is located at aboveground level, requiring the first retail level to be about 12 feet above the street.

Retail stores are located on the first, second and third levels above the parking. The multiscreen theater stretches over four floors (levels two through five). A food court is located on the third shopping level. A music court is the main attraction on the fourth shopping level, and a discotheque dominates the fifth, where revelers can party atop the flat roof. The seven levels are linked through stairs, elevators and escalators. The eateries and entertainment functions account for 60

MAJOR TENANTS		
NAME	TYPE	GLA (SQ. FT.)
Warner Lusomundo	Multiscreen theater	19,950
Markesina	Nightclub/discotheque	14,615
Automáticos Canarios	Family-entertainment center	7,362
Zara	Apparel	6,479
Sfera-El Corte Inglés	Apparel	3,746
C&A	Apparel	3,510
Cortefiel	Apparel	2,952

A multilevel graphic (left) lists the center's major tenants. A sculpture (below) of a whale's tale accents the seaside location.

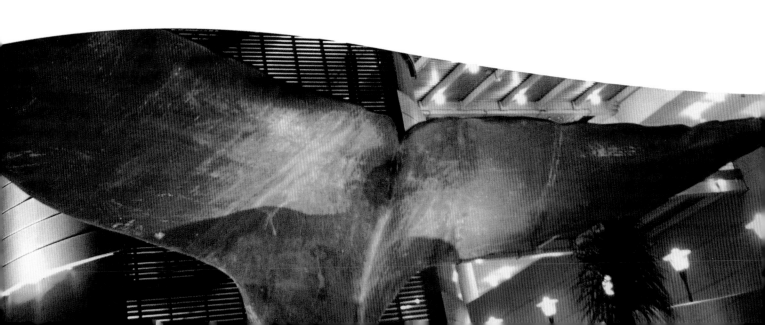

Shopowners
design their own
storefronts and
signs (above and
below).

*Materials used in
the exterior
construction are
both attractive
and durable
enough to resist
marine abrasion
(above).*

*Extensive use of
glass makes for
true transparency
at El Muelle.*

percent of the occupied square footage. Shopowners were free to design their own storefronts and signs, as long as materials were of good quality.

Exterior coloration took into account the natural surroundings. The facade of the four-level cinema complex reflects the leaden gray sky of Las Palmas. At night, lighthouse towers and terraces provide a landmark on the city skyline. Artificial "lakes" were placed on the sides of the center facing the city, giving the impression that El Muelle rises from the sea.

Materials used in exterior construction had to be both attractive and durable, containing a high level of resistance to marine abrasion. A major complication during the construction phase came from the island location: orders had to be placed well in advance, particularly since some items, like the Italian facade panels, came from great distances. Strikes in the port and complex stockpiling of supplies in the limited space also proved challenging.

The wave-like canopy and imposing lighthouse towers have become landmarks in the night sky.

Beyond the artificial lakes, landscaping included appropriate amounts of vegetation, cybernetic fountains and sculpture. The seven-level structure required attention to exit routes for shoppers. These were concentrated in two tower stairwells that became visual landmarks to the rest of the city.

The building has a reinforced concrete structure, with two-directional floor structures made with box formwork. Metal structure has also been used for the volume of the cinemas and the large canopy crowning the center, which is wave-shaped, further linking the design to the seaside setting.

Inside, the color tones are those of the surrounding sea — shades of blue and white, accented by dark-blue columns stretching upwards for the five retail floors. There is extensive use of shaded glass, uniting the center with surrounding neighborhoods. One of the most striking design aspects is the center's transparency — window walls allow passersby to have a clear view of shopping activity and graphics inside the center.

Even strolling toward the center, shoppers have plenty to look at.

El Muelle needed a striking design, inasmuch as there are six other shopping centers in close proximity. The sea-themed design and high priority on entertainment, however, have established El Muelle as a desirable destination.

The center's seven levels are linked through stairs, elevators and escalators.

Inside El Muelle, shades of blue and azure dominate the design and complement the island ambience.

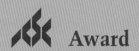

Hoshigaoka Terrace
Nagoya, Aichi Prefecture, Japan

Owner:
Higashiyama Yuen Co., Ltd.
Nagoya, Aichi Prefecture, Japan

Management Company:
Higashiyama Yuen Co., Ltd.
Nagoya, Aichi Prefecture, Japan
and
TECH R&DS Co., Ltd.
Tokyo, Tokyo Prefecture, Japan

Design Architect and Graphic Designer:
Gensler
San Francisco, California, United States

Production Architect:
TECH R&DS Co., Ltd.
Tokyo, Tokyo Prefecture, Japan
and
Takenaka Corporation
Nagoya, Aichi Prefecture, Japan

Lighting Designer:
Rise Co., Ltd./D-Brain Corporation
Osaka, Osaka Prefecture, Japan

Landscape Architect:
Ohtori Consultants/D-Brain Corporation
Osaka, Osaka Prefecture, Japan

General Contractor:
Takenaka Corporation
Nagoya, Aichi Prefecture, Japan

Development Company:
Higashiyama Yuen Co., Ltd.
Nagoya, Aichi Prefecture, Japan

Leasing Company:
TECH R&DS Co., Ltd.
Tokyo, Tokyo Prefecture, Japan

Gross size of center:
140,943 sq. ft.

**Gross leasable area
(small shop space, excluding anchors):**
102,701 sq. ft.

Total acreage of site:
7.1 acres

Type of center:
Neighborhood/community lifestyle center

Physical description:
Four-level open mall

Center's trade area:
Suburban

Population:
- Primary trading area
  454,962

- Secondary trading area
  579,213

- Annualized percentage of shoppers
  anticipated to be from outside trade area
  5%

Development schedule:
- Original opening date
  March 20, 2003

Parking spaces:
- Present number
  1,500, in two parking structures

*Pedestrians at
Hoshigaoka Terrace
in Nagoya, Japan,
pass the Gap as they
enter the project.*

*I*n crowded Japan, one must often work around existing structures to develop new projects. At Hoshigaoka Terrace in Nagoya, this was literally true — the four-level open-air lifestyle center is bisected lengthwise by a sloping street. The mall is also closely surrounded by five other buildings: two parking lots, a department store, a bowling alley and an apartment building with ground-floor retail. One goal of the project was to knit these disparate elements together, yet establish Hoshigaoka Terrace as a distinct retail destination.

The east side of the project cuts into a hillside and climbs four terraced levels. Each of the terraced levels is visually and literally accessible via the Grand Stairs, an amphitheater-style element designed both to entertain and circulate shoppers throughout the center. The Grand Stairs encompasses the Theatre Plaza, which is the main open space on the east side.

Photograph: Takenaka Corporation/Yukio Yoshimura

The Four Seasons Plaza, on the project's east side, offers garden seating near stores.

Across Hoshigaokamotomachi Street, the west side of the project incorporates the sloping roadway into its architectural design. An upper-level walkway uses open space to create the Four Seasons Plaza, a series of gently sloping gardens and courts facing the retail shops. Floor levels change subtly from shop to shop, making a smooth transition up the slope to the existing street.

Photograph: Takenaka Corporation/Kenzou Aoyama

Photograph: Takenaka Corporation/Yukio Yoshimura

Aerial views show the unusual layout of the mall, with Hoshigaokamotomachi Street bisecting the project from north to south. Pedestrian bridges (above and right) aid shopper circulation.

Photograph: Nacása & Partner Inc./Atsushi Nakamichi

The flow of customer traffic was a major concern in the planning process. The site climbs 30 feet over the length of the property from north to south, parallel to Hoshigaokamotomachi Street.

Pedestrians coming to the project from the north start a loop at Level 1 (the street level adjacent to the apartment building and one of the neighboring stores). They pass entrances to the Gap and Starbucks. Moving up the slope, they pass restaurants and the Four Seasons Plaza, lined with shops. At the top, they arrive at Level 2, which connects with another neighboring store and parking. Shoppers cross the Theatre Plaza at the base of the Grand Stairs and

Photograph: Takenaka Corporation/Yukio Yoshimura

The center at night (above) shows the roof over a curved walkway, where shoppers can see the east side. The east side center mall itself (below), facing south.

Photograph: Nacása & Partner Inc./Atsushi Nakamichi

Steps double as amphitheater seating (above) on the project's east side. A walkway (below right) crosses Hoshigaokamotomachi Street and leads to the Gap anchor. A blue Japanese sky bathes the sloped upper walkway (below) on the west side.

Photograph: Takenaka Corporation/Kenzou Aoyama

Photograph: Takenaka Corporation/Kenzou Aoyama

enter an open-air walkway that leads past a variety of shops to the pedestrian bridge, which in turns takes shoppers to the project's west side. Once there, they walk along a curving balcony lined with retail, where they can enjoy views to the open space below. By sound placement of stores, restaurants, plazas, courts and gardens, the project achieved a progression of circulation elements and open spaces that establishes a cohesive sense of place.

Both design and leasing took into

Photograph: Nacása & Partner Inc./Atsushi Nakamichi

Photograph: Takenaka Corporation/Kenzou Aoyama

Photograph: Nacása & Partner Inc./Atsushi Nakamichi

Photograph: Takenaka Corporation/Kenzou Aoyama

Families (top) are attracted by the mix of retail, eateries and entertainment. Apparel stores, such as Armani Jeans and Belle Boudoir (above) and Laura Ashley (right), have a strong presence at Hoshigaoka Terrace.

account the neighborhood's preponderance of young families. Families can follow some shopping time with a quick walk to the adjacent bowling alley. Nearly a dozen food establishments add appeal for families.

The developers, who are based in Nagoya as well, felt the need to do something exceptional with this project in their home city. Shopping, they knew, is a social act, and retail settings are an important way to experience the city as a community. By sponsoring a design that goes beyond mere shopping to create major public spaces, the developers of Hoshigaoka Terrace created an integral place in the city.

A fragrance shop storefront calls to a young shopper on the west side.

Photograph: Takenaka Corporation/Kenzou Aoyama

MAJOR TENANTS

NAME	TYPE	GLA (SQ. FT.)
Gap/GapKids	Apparel	12,647
UFJ Bank	Financial institution	11,979
MUJI (Mujirushi Ryohin)	Lifestyle merchandiser	8,527
Laura Ashley	Apparel	4,185
Hush Hush	Apparel	3,584

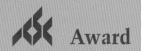
The Mall at Millenia

Orlando, Florida, United States

Owners:
The Forbes Company
Southfield, Michigan, United States
and
Taubman Centers, Inc.
Bloomfield Hills, Michigan, United States

Management Company:
The Forbes Company
Southfield, Michigan, United States

Design and Production Architect and Graphic Designer:
JPRA Architects
Farmington Hills, Michigan, United States

Lighting Designer:
Focus Lighting Inc.
New York, New York, United States

Landscape Architect:
Grissim Metz Associates
Farmington Hills, Michigan, United States

General Contractor:
Hardin Construction Company, LLC
Tampa, Florida, United States

Development and Leasing Companies:
The Forbes Company
Southfield, Michigan, United States
and
Taubman Centers, Inc.
Bloomfield Hills, Michigan, United States

Gross size of center:
1.4 million sq. ft.

**Gross leasable area
(small shop space, excluding anchors):**
524,500 sq. ft., plus 790-seat food court

Total acreage of site:
87 acres

Type of center:
Super-regional retail center

Physical description:
Enclosed two-level mall

Center's trade area:
Suburban

Population:
* Primary trading area
  1.7 million

* Annualized percentage of shoppers
  anticipated to be from outside trade area
  50%

Development schedule:
* Opening date
  October 18, 2002

Parking spaces:
* Parking on grade
  5,430

*Palm trees and a
56-foot-high circular
glass rotunda frame
the lower-level Water
Garden entry at The
Mall at Millenia in
Orlando, Florida.*

Geometry informs the design of The Mall at Millenia, a two-level enclosed mall in Orlando, Florida. The center's architectural envelope and interior spaces rely on forms of the circle, square and triangle, giving the overall project an international contemporary style. The building design blends bold use of exposed steel and stainless steel with glass, stone and wood.

Perhaps the most recognizable architectural feature is its curved S-shaped 63-foot-high vaulted skylight that soars above the main concourse and its four elliptical courts. Natural light floods the space by day and is replaced at night with special lighting that showcases design features. The curved mall area allows for a variety of tenant depths while keeping an overall rectangular structural envelope. The 400-foot mall area

The most striking design component (above) is the S-shaped roof skylight. The upper-level Winter Garden entry (right) is a triangular 41-foot-high lobby.

is uninterrupted by stores — the two largest anchors, Bloomingdale's and Macy's, are at either end of the mall, and the third, smaller anchor, Neiman Marcus, connects through a court area where the curve is closest to the building perimeter.

There are two main entrances, the Winter Garden and the Water Garden, both of which are monumental in scale. The lower-level Water Garden entry has a 56-foot-high circular glass rotunda. Its theme of "universe, earth and time" is carried through in programmed lighting and fountain features. The upper-level Winter Garden is a 41-foot-high glass triangular lobby. An orange orchard rises above shoppers' heads in nine planters, which themselves feature 27 bas-relief sculptural panels of garden life. Undulating benches suggest Florida's ever-present water, while pinpoint lights at the ceiling suggest a starry Florida night. Palm trees are used in interior plantings.

Palm and orange trees have their place at The Mall at Millenia. In the Winter Garden (above), an orange orchard grows from triangular planters. Outside (left), native palms grace a curved and shaved-glass awning.

The mall's Grand Court — 120 feet in diameter — is circled by 12 masts, each 35 feet high, with graphics relating to a calendar month. Each mast contains a poetic narrative etched in glass, describing the significance of the month. The masts also support 12 LED screens (IMAX format) for live and taped video displays with sound, which provide information on fashion and culture to shoppers. The floor of the Grand Court has a graphic that is 60 feet in diameter. In it, swirling leaves diminish in size as they approach a central point, only to emerge as sea life in the form of fish completing a metamorphosis story from "Sea to Earth." The silver-green terrazzo leaves and fish are bordered with stainless-steel trim, all set within a deep sea-green epoxy terrazzo field.

Geometry is everywhere. Oval lighting fixtures and circular seating areas are used (left) in a court, while the barrel skylight and a triangular balcony (below) are suspended over a mall area elsewhere.

IMAX LED displays provide entertainment and information to shoppers at the Grand Court, with its terrazzo graphic.

The Orangerie Cafes, located in the Winter Garden, is a group of 12 restaurants with a common dining area for over 790 people. Its design includes a contemporary skylit dining space, illuminated frosted-glass columns, white terrazzo flooring and detailed furnishings. A children's play area is centrally located on a platform within the café area.

Florida's bright light and heat drew attention in the design process. Glass is abundant in the project, even beyond the S-shaped barrel-vaulted skylight. Solar loads were mitigated to meet energy-code requirements by layering three colors of tinted glass

MAJOR TENANTS		
NAME	TYPE	GLA (SQ. FT.)
Macy's	Department store	275,000
Bloomingdale's	Department store	235,000
Neiman Marcus	Department store	90,000

The Grand Court (above left) features the months of the year in a floor graphic. The Orangerie (left) offers eateries with seating (above right) for nearly 800 shoppers.

in the skylights. While lighting fixtures are used for dramatic effect throughout the 60-foot-high mall area, 80 percent of the fixtures can be reached without special lifts.

The mall is in one of the most competitive entertainment arenas in the world, just 10 miles from Disney World, two miles from Universal Studios and close to many other attractions, all of which bring visitors from around the globe. The tenant mix, containing a range of first-time retailers and restaurants as well as such internationally known names as Burberry, Gap, Tiffany & Co. and Gucci, blends with the contemporary design to place The Mall at Millenia among the must-see visits for locals and tourists alike.

The Orangerie offers poetic thoughts to diners (left), who may also encounter this column bathed in aquatic tones in the Water Court (right).

 **Award**

The Market Common, Clarendon

Arlington, Virginia, United States

Owner:
**Clarendon Edgewood 10, LLC;
CoPERA, RREEF, McCaffery Interests**
Chicago, Illinois, United States

Management Company:
RREEF and McCaffery Interests
Chicago, Illinois, United States

Design and Production Architect:
Antunovich Associates
Chicago, Illinois, United States

Graphic Design:
McG Studios
McG Studios
Boulder, Colorado, United States

Landscape Architect:
Jacobs/Ryan Associates
Chicago, Illinois, United States

General Contractor:
Hensel Phelps/Plan, a Joint Venture
San Francisco, California, United States

Development and Leasing Company:
McCaffery Interests, Inc.
Chicago, Illinois, United States

Gross size of center:
1,232,181 sq. ft.

Gross leasable area
(small shop space, excluding anchors):
303,150 sq. ft.

Total acreage of site:
17.87 acres

Type of center:
Mixed-use lifestyle center

Physical description:
Open mall

Center's trade area:
Urban but not Central Business District

Population:
• Primary trading area
  42,000

• Secondary trading area
  680,000

• Annualized percentage of shoppers
  anticipated to be from outside trade area
  20%

Development schedule:
• Original opening dates
  November 2001 (Phase I) and
  November 2003 (Phases II and III)

Parking spaces
• Present number
  1,310

*The courtyard at
The Market
Common, Clarendon
adds community
space to the urban-
style retail setting.*

*T*he Market Common, Clarendon is a mixed-use development on 18 acres in the Washington, DC, suburb of Arlington, Virginia. The property was surrounded by a dense assortment of single-family neighborhoods that had been part of a traditional shopping and restaurant area that had fallen into decline. The project, carried out in three phases, encompasses office space,

Photograph: Duane Lempke, Sisson Studios, Inc.

Photograph: Duane Lempke, Sisson Studios, Inc.

MAJOR TENANTS		
NAME	**TYPE**	**GLA (SQ. FT.)**
Crate & Barrel	Home	36,875
The Container Store	Home	29,994
Barnes & Noble Booksellers	Books/music	27,000
Pottery Barn	Home	16,924
The Cheesecake Factory	Restaurant	12,598

An aerial view (left) shows that the stores surrounding the courtyard are themselves surrounded by residential space alongside and atop. Crate & Barrel (below) is one of the home-focused retailers that make an attractive retail mix for the neighborhood.

Photograph: Duane Lempke, Sisson Studios, Inc.

retail and restaurant space, for-lease housing and for-sale housing, along with surface and structured parking and open parklands.

All three phases involved property with frontage along major arterial streets. Phase I included 87 for-sale town houses, a new one-acre neighborhood park and a mixed-use urban village with 300 rental apartments above 210,000 square feet of retail and restaurants. The shops and eateries wrap around a central courtyard containing water features, public art, a playground and landscaped areas. An internal street links the courtyard with a city boulevard. Phases II and III added 55,000 square feet of retail and restaurant space. All phases added parking to the neighborhood.

Photograph: Duane Lempke, Sisson Studios, Inc.

The development (above) kept on-street parking available to the residents. Water features (below) provide sights and sounds that accompany shopping at dusk.

Photograph: Duane Lempke, Sisson Studios, Inc.

Photograph: Duane Lempke, Sisson Studios, Inc.

Rental units are located over storefronts at The Market Common, Clarendon.

Although there was no public financing involved in the project, the development team saw the value in creating a strong partnership with neighborhood groups over time. There had been an earlier bitter proposal to build a "big-box" project. The developer encountered a difficult and distrusting community response at first, and held a series of over 40 meetings with community groups. In the end, one nearby resident remarked, "When we first saw the plan for The Market Common, we said, 'Oh, there goes the neighborhood.' When the development was completed and we saw how McCaffery had lived up to its promises, we said, 'Here comes the neighborhood.' "

The design has an urban feel, emphasizing retail at the street level and the residential component on upper levels, yet the courtyard, extensive landscaping, water features and wide brick sidewalks encourage pedestrian use. The tenant mix focuses heavily on home products. Anchor stores include The Container Store, Crate & Barrel and Pottery Barn. Nearly three dozen other stores are represented, including restaurants, apparel and service stores.

Brick-paved walkways, benches, a playground and fountains bring a park-like ambience to the project.

Building exteriors were kept within a color palette of tans and whites, with accents from earth tones. Brick and other materials are carefully patterned to maintain visual interest. Benches, handrails, streetlights and planters each reflect attention to design, which is further enhanced by cupolas and rooftop moldings at the highest points in the project.

The process of balancing the various property uses, interests of multiple owners (including the town house developer), consultants and contractors proved challenging to the development team. In the end, however, The Market Common satisfied the need for a town center for the Clarendon neighborhood and became a catalyst for the area's rebirth, spurring over $1 billion in new neighborhood development.

Photographs: Duane Lempke, Sisson Studios, Inc.

Whimsical sculpture highlights a fieldstone multilevel fountain (left and below).

Photograph: Duane Lempke, Sisson Studios, Inc.

Photograph: Duane Lempke, Sisson Studios, Inc.

Rooftop moldings, cupolas and outdoor dining areas bring visual interest to the upper levels of The Market Common, Clarendon.

Photograph: Duane Lempke, Sisson Studios, Inc.

Altmarkt-Galerie Dresden

Dresden, Germany

Owner Company:
Altmarkt-Galerie Dresden KG
Dresden, Germany

Management Company:
ECE Projektmanagement G.m.b.H. & Co. KG
Hamburg, Germany

Design and Production Architect:
Jost Hering; Hans Martin Hoffmann
Hamburg, Germany
In cooperation with
Prof. Dip.I-Ing. Manfred Schomers and Dipl.-Ing. Rainer Schürmann

Lighting Designer:
Bartenbach Lichtlabor
Innsbruck, Austria

Landscape Architect:
Noack Landschaftsarchitekten
Dresden, Germany

Development and Leasing Company:
ECE Projektmanagement G.m.B.H. & Co. KG
Hamburg, Germany

Gross size of center:
279,864 sq. ft.

**Gross leasable area
(small shop space, excluding anchors):**
96,876 sq. ft.

Type of center:
Inner-city shopping center

Physical description:
Enclosed three-level mall

Location of trading area:
Urban Central Business District

Population:
- Primary trading area
  180,000

- Secondary trading area
  780,000

- Annualized percentage of shoppers
  anticipated to be from outside trade area
  approximately 15%

Development schedule:
- Original opening date
  September 18, 2002

Parking spaces:
- Present number
  520

The Altmarkt-Galerie Dresden is a three-level mall in the central trade area of Dresden – a modern shopping center in a historic district on Germany's eastern border.

There are three square buildings that take up the historical Gassenviertel, or alleyways. The buildings are arranged in a north-to-south direction following the layout of the Webergasse and the Zahnsgasse, which were destroyed during World War II. These alleys, with their arched facades, act both as street areas (using the stone

coverings of the outside facade) and as interior space (with a shed-roof glass construction at about 45 feet high). The three levels are linked by elevators and escalators and are served by a one-level underground garage for 520 vehicles.

The Webergasse, a public passage between two streets, can now be totally closed in the winter. Two glass roofs connect the new building with the surrounding block. Free space between the old and new buildings has been designed as high-class squares.

The building's exterior is divided into stone fronts and transparent-glass surfaces for shop windows. Exterior design features include point-held glazing of the first-floor glass elements and loggias with metallic light palms as well as

fine-cut portals.

Once inside, the historic ambience gives way to modern design. Rotundas and courts are clad with two-piece finished parts, slightly profiled and arched inwards. Hanging bridges connect the three buildings above the alleys. Water features are placed between escalators. Abundant natural light showers all three shopping levels. A glass lodge containing a café/bistro occupies one building entrance.

Timeworn facades (right) remind shoppers of the historic context of the Altmarkt-Galerie in Dresden, Germany. Bridges (above) connect the three main buildings in the project.

Large plazas (above) are located between historic buildings and the mall's new ones.

There are over 100 shops, ranging from gifts and a supermarket to designer fashions and consumer electronics. Cafés, restaurants and services occupy over 20,000 square feet, with another 50,000 square feet on the third and fourth floors leased as office space.

The project incorporates many historic components. A cellar vault from the 13th century was assigned to a wine dealer — a glass cube above allows shoppers to look into the vault. Next to the cube are two models of the city, one showing the area before the destruction of 1945, the other as the city is now. Findings from archaeological excavations and stones from the site are exhibited in wire baskets. The city planning department, the state archaeology authority and the state office for

Bare metal (above) is a neutral design presence, complementing both old and new looks.

protection of monuments worked closely with the developer throughout the project.

Promotion of the center ties in with that of the city. The center's management team organizes marketing activities and campaigns both for the mall and for the city as a whole. Several surveys have shown that the Altmarkt-Galerie has enhanced the city's attractiveness as a tourist destination.

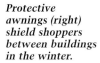

Protective awnings (right) shield shoppers between buildings in the winter.

MAJOR TENANTS

NAME	TYPE	GLA (SQ. FT.)
Saturn	Consumer electronics	64,584
Sinn Leffers	Fashion	53,820
SportScheck	Sports	32,292
Hugendubel	Books	17,224

Once inside Altmarkt-Galerie (left and right), historic ambience gives way to modern design.

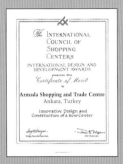

Armada Shopping and Trade Centre

Ankara, Turkey

Owner:
Sogutozu Construction and Management Inc.
Ankara, Turkey

Management Company:
Armada Management and Trade Inc.
Ankara, Turkey

Design Architect:
GMW Architecture and Consulting Ltd. Co.
London, United Kingdom

Production and Landscape Architect:
Ali Osman Ozturk/A Tasarim Architecture and Consulting Ltd. Co.
Ankara, Turkey

Graphic and Lighting Designer:
Vecihi Yildiz
Ankara, Turkey

General Contractor and Development Company:
Sogutozu Construction and Management Inc.
Ankara, Turkey

Leasing Company:
Avi Alkas/Alkas Shopping Centre Consulting Ltd. Co.
Istanbul, Turkey

Gross size of center:
1,076,426 sq. ft.

**Gross leasable area
(small shop space, excluding anchors):**
337,277 sq. ft.

Total acreage of site:
7.4 acres

Type of center:
Regional center

Physical description:
Enclosed mall

Location of trading area:
Urban Central Business District

Population:
- Primary trading area
  534,109
- Secondary trading area
  1,000,000
- Annualized percentage of shoppers anticipated to be from outside trade area
  10%

Development schedule:
- Original opening date
  September 28, 2002

Parking spaces:
- Present number
  3,000

*A*rmada Shopping and Trade Centre is a six-story shopping center that is virtually a city-within-a-city, clad in over 160,000 square feet of glass. Within the complex are 153 shops, 21 restaurants and 11 movie theaters. The center sits alongside a 21-story office building. "Armada" means the flagship of a naval flotilla and is appropriate, given the ship-like shapes of the office tower and the mall block.

The project presented two challenges. First was the site's natural slope — over 30 feet from one end to the other. Second, but equally daunting, were the restrictions placed on the project by the municipal government.

Armada's sloping issue was solved by increasing the number of mall entrances — shoppers can enter from four sides at three different elevations: on the back side at the hypermarket level, two on the long sides of the first basement level and a main entrance on the ground floor. This arrangement allows cars (parked on all four sides) to be close to entries.

The Armada Shopping and Trade Centre's mall block and office tower are visible from most of Ankara, Turkey.

The municipal regulations concerned space use – net floor area to lot area, distances to neighboring lots and roads, and so on. When an initial design followed the regulations, the result was a low, wide, hangar-like building, similar to that envisioned by the investors. The architect, however, convinced them of the value of vertical construction – a low mall block with a slender office tower. Inasmuch as the lot is visible from most of Ankara, the new plot plan makes the site a visual landmark.

The tenant mix is upscale and 23 retailers have located their first stores at Ankara. Each shop is placed in a specified area. The hypermarket floor offers service establishments. The lower floor focuses on goods for children, home decoration, music and books and personal-care products. Apparel, jewelry, shoe and sports stores are on upper floors. A food court offers 21 fast-food units of national and international appeal.

Armada maintains a strong public-service presence. Fund-raising

A towering entryway (above) welcomes shoppers.

A severely sloping lot caused the planning team to site entries at three levels, which helps shopper traffic circulate throughout the six retail levels.

events have included those for homeless children's school needs, leukemia, rest-home residents and university scholarships. The economic presence is even more powerful — a trade group's survey showed that retail sales in the city of Ankara increased 10% with the opening of Armada Shopping and Trade Centre.

Armada gets its name from a key naval vessel, prompted from the ship-like exterior of the shopping mall (right).

Gleaming interior surfaces accent retail areas, a food court, service establishments and the cinema level at Armada Shopping and Trade Centre.

MAJOR TENANTS

NAME	TYPE	GLA (SQ. FT.)
Gima	Supermarket	37,115
Tuze Armada	Cinema	32,293
Beymen	Department store	18,622
Vakko	Department store	18,515
Carsi	Department store	12,874

The Ferry Building Marketplace

San Francisco, California, United States

Owner:
Port of San Francisco
San Francisco, California, United States

Joint Developers:
Equity Office Properties Trust
Wilson Meany Sullivan LLC
Primus Infrastructure LLC
San Francisco, California, United States

Architect:
SMWM
San Francisco, California, United States

Retail Architect:
Baldauf Catton von Eckartsberg Architects
San Francisco, California, United States

Preservation Architect:
Page & Turnbull
San Francisco, California, United States

Architect, Port Commission Hearing Room:
Tom Eliot Fisch
San Francisco, California, United States

Lighting Design:
Horton Lees Brogden
San Francisco, California, United States

Building Signage Design:
Arias Associates
San Francisco, California, United States

General Contractor:
Plant Construction Company
San Francisco, California, United States

Gross size of center:
65,000 sq. ft.

Gross leasable area
(small shop space, excluding anchors):
65,000 sq. ft.

Total acreage of site:
2.65 acres

Type of center:
Multiuse historic office and retail marketplace

Physical description:
Enclosed and open-air marketplace

Location of trading area:
Urban Central Business District

Population:
• Primary trading area
  750,000

• Secondary trading area
  6,700,000

• Annualized percentage of shoppers
  anticipated to be from outside trade area
  20%

Development schedule:
• Original opening date
  March 2003

Parking:
Multiple local parking options available
seven days a week

*The Ferry Building
old (upper right) and
new (right).*

The Ferry Building Marketplace is part of a multiuse waterfront complex that gave new life to one of San Francisco's best-known edifices.

For more than a century, the Ferry Building had been a much-loved landmark. Opened in 1898, the Beaux Arts building was the primary point of arrivals and departures for San Francisco until the construction of the Golden Gate and Bay Bridges in the late 1930s. In 1957, erection of the Embarcadero Freeway literally overshadowed the Ferry Building. When the 1989 Loma Prieta earthquake forced removal of the freeway, the door opened to rehabilitation of the landmark.

The public space of the original building was on the second floor, with the ticketing hall downstairs. The new design turned the first floor into the focal point and cut significant openings to the two-story Nave above, creating a naturally lit dramatic three-story space for the public galleria.

Photograph: © California Historical Society

Photograph: © Richard Barnes

Photograph: © Tom Paiva

The Nave at The Ferry Building Marketplace under construction (above) and loaded with shops and shoppers (right).

Photograph: © Richard Barnes

The ground floor of the renovated Ferry Building became a 65,000-square-foot retail marketplace showcasing the fine restaurants and food producers of the Bay Area. The Marketplace is organized along the Nave, an indoor street that runs the entire 660-foot length of the building. Restaurants and cafés anchor three corners of the ground floor and offer sweeping views of the city and the bay. Along the Nave, retail shops ranging in size from 260 square feet to over 5,000 square feet offer locally

grown food products and related food, wine and cooking goods.

Across the Nave from the arcades, two Market Halls feature a cluster of specialty shops offering quality meats, poultry and charcuterie. Two outdoor arcades provide a permanent home for the Ferry Plaza Farmers' Market.

In creating a vibrant and original setting, the architects and designers were nonetheless reverential to the rich history of the building

The Ferry Building Marketplace unites many types of local food producers with city residents and tourists seeking the finest ingredients.

Photograph: © Richard Barnes

Photograph: © David Wakely

Photograph: © David Wakely

as designed by A. Page Brown and worked to preserve and embrace the building's historical quality.

Some aspects of the project were modeled on the European experience, and the designers studied such successes as the Parisian street markets, Harrods in London and Peck in Milan, as well as the Pike Place Market in Seattle. The Marketplace also kept the European tradition of offering two of each type of food specialty store — two butchers, two olive oil vendors, two fish stores, and the like.

Locals and tourists are flocking to the project, which unites the great orchards of the South Bay, the dairies of Marin and the vineyards of Napa and Sonoma. Thanks to its new location, the Farmers' Market attendance has grown from 5,000 to 8,000 on weekdays and from 10,000 to over 20,000 on Saturdays. The original purpose of the property receives its due as well, since use of the ferry itself has increased more than 12% overall, and is up 27% on weekends.

Photograph: © BCV Architects

Photograph: © BCV Architects

Photograph: © BCV Architects

Photograph: © BCV Architects

MAJOR TENANTS

NAME	TYPE	GLA (SQ. FT.)
The Ferry Plaza Farmers' Market	Farm Produce	7,677
Taylor's Refresher	Restaurant	3,433
Acme Bread Company	Breads/baked goods	2,552
Ferry Plaza Seafood	Eatery/seafood	1,493
Mijita Taqueria	Eatery	1,380
Hog Island Oyster Company	Eatery/seafood	1,016

The varied smells of a bakery (lower left) and a fish eatery (lower right) add to the sensory experience of a visit to The Ferry Building Marketplace.

Photograph: © David Wakely

Photograph: © David Wakely

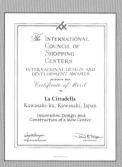

La Cittadella

Kawasaki-ku, Kawasaki, Japan

Owner and Management Company:
Citta' Entertainment Co., Ltd.
Kawasaki-ku, Kawasaki, Japan

Design Architect:
The Jerde Partnership
Venice, California, United States

Production Architect:
Ishimoto Architects
Tokyo, Japan

Graphic Design:
Selbert Perkins Design
Plaza Del Rey, California, United States

Lighting Designer:
Kaplan Partners Architectural Lighting
Los Angeles, California, United States

Landscape Architect:
EDAW
Los Angeles, California, United States

General Contractor:
Obayashi Corporation
Tokyo, Japan

Development and Leasing Company:
Citta' Entertainment Co., Ltd.
Kawasaki-ku, Kawasaki, Japan

Gross size of center:
255,000 sq. ft.

**Gross leasable area
(small shop space, excluding anchors):**
55,000 sq. ft.

Total acreage of site:
4 acres

Type of center:
Community lifestyle center

Physical description:
Four-floor open-air town center

Location of trading area:
Urban but not Central Business District

Population:
- Primary trading area
  1,460,000

- Secondary trading area
  2,700,000

- Annualized percentage of shoppers
  anticipated to be from outside trade area
  15%

Development schedule:
- Original opening date
  November 24, 2002

Parking spaces:
- Present number
  500

*La Cittadella is a
four-level shopping
and entertainment
center.*

Building in Japan means limited space, and the developers of La Cittadella — an entertainment center in densely populated Kawasaki — wanted to avoid stacking floors atop each other in a rectangular box.

The solution was to build a terraced village inspired by the hill towns of Italy. The visual look is striking, which was important to the goals of city planners, who wanted to give a face-lift to Kawasaki's profile as an industrial port city.

Italy or Japan? La Cittadella in Kawasaki, Japan, uses Italianate design. A 250-seat amphitheater (left) is a centerpiece of the project.

La Cittadella is a shopping and entertainment complex that includes dining, a 13-screen cinema and the relocation of the 80-year-old Club Citta'. Shopping is centered in the "Italian village" retail area. All restaurants have outdoor seating, also reflective of the Italianate concept. The center of the project is a 250-seat sunken amphitheater sunk eight feet below ground; it is animated by water, light and sound.

Visitors stroll along 15-foot-wide gently sloping streets that meander upward and switch back on themselves. The resulting terraces form a hillside — an unusual site in the otherwise flat city of Kawasaki. The streets pass shops, cafés and restaurants to reach the upper-level entertainment district. Two pedestrian bridges also connect to the upper level. La Cittadella is designed to draw visitors upward, so they reach the top without knowing quite how they got there.

Textured paving, ornate streetlamps and unboxy structures add to the Italian feel of the site.

MAJOR TENANTS		
NAME	**TYPE**	**GLA (SQ. FT.)**
Cinecitta'	Cinema complex	108,400
Club Citta'	Live hall	30,500
Comme CA Market	Market	9,752
Game Pia	Videogame store	9,623
Tower Records	Music store	9,060

An important aspect of the entertainment district was the relocation of the historic and famed Club Citta' within the site and building the lifestyle components around it. The mix works — for example, the 13-screen cinema now captures 80% of the community's filmgoing market, even after a competing state-of-the-art theater opened nearby.

Rich colors and textures are layered with aesthetic landscaping and water features. The buildings vary in height and have windows scaled like those in residential areas – giving a true community look to what is nonetheless a retail center. The color palette is comprised of warm earth tones — cream, tan and brick — further emphasizing the Italianate image. Lighting is used dramatically at night to differentiate the two sections. In the retail center, illumination is subtle and white. In the entertainment area, lighting is bold and colored.

Its developers believe that the project challenges accepted thinking about tenant visibility, circulation, flat-level retail and rigid tenant configurations. La Cittadella is a significant step in the city planners' efforts to introduce "bright and clean urban space" into Kawasaki — the start of a complete rejuvenation of the area.

A water feature accents the amphitheater (above) at La Cittadella. The terraced layout of the circulation path results in a hillside that starkly contrasts with the flat city itself.

Wide plazas, curved facades and narrow walkways (below and right) reinforce the Italian design concept of the retail/entertainment complex La Cittadella.

Les Passages de l'Hôtel de Ville

Boulogne-Billancourt, France

Owner:
CECOBIL (AXA Reim France/Klépierre)
Paris, France

Management Company:
Ségécé
Paris, France

Design/Production/Graphic Architect:
Dusapin & Leclercq
Paris, France

Landscape Architect:
Blanc (interior) and Chetietov (exterior)
Paris, France

General Contractor:
GEC
Paris, France

Development and Leasing Company:
Ségécé
Paris, France

Gross size of center:
275,436 sq. ft.

**Gross leasable area
(small shop space, excluding anchors):**
90,700 sq. ft.

Total acreage of site:
16.1 acres

Type of center:
Community lifestyle center

Physical description:
Partially enclosed mall

Location of trading area:
Urban Central Business District

Population:
- Primary trading area
  148,000

- Secondary trading area
  147,000

- Annualized percentage of shoppers
  anticipated to be from outside trade area
  0%

Development schedule:
- Original opening date
  May 31, 2004

Parking spaces:
- Present number
  600

Les Passages de l'Hôtel de Ville is a central element in the urban redevelopment program of Boulogne-Billancourt, a western suburb of Paris. The urban fabric of Boulogne-Billancourt is a patchwork of interconnected, fiercely independent districts, cut through by busy thoroughfares. There was no "center" unifying the town.

The project created a town center, building on the Parisian tradition of comfortable, busy arcades blending in with their urban surroundings. It also renovated the urban fabric of the district, which had been a hodgepodge of run-down areas. The redevelopment program included residences (including student housing), office space, a seven-screen cinema, a child-care center, boutiques, restaurants, parking and a large public square. Two newly created roads provide access to the shopping center — one is a landscaped pedestrian zone.

Inside the center, the mall area is a stark double-height glass-roofed atrium, softened by wooden pan-

The central design component of Les Passages de l'Hôtel de Ville is the 721-foot-long mall area, topped by a glass canopy.

Design of the mall area sought to blend the mall with surrounding shopping streets.

MAJOR TENANTS		
NAME	**TYPE**	**GLA (SQ. FT.)**
Fnac	Leisure	38,996
Inno Gourmet	Supermarket	38,118
Zara	Apparel	23,596
Go Sport	Leisure	18,969

els and fluid, simple lighting. The mall area is 721 feet long, 32 feet high and ranges from 20 feet to 40 feet wide. On the ground, there are two lateral gray granite strips, evoking the external treatment of the walkways, containing patterned marble brought from Italy, Greece and Turkey.

Overall, the design blends Les Passages de l'Hôtel de Ville with the surrounding shopping blocks. A creative interpretation of the standard materials found on any urban street informed the choice of contemporary and sophisticated materials such as glass, metal and stone. On the upper floors, shutters and candelabra-style lighting hide all technical components of the project from public view.

Parking got special attention. The garage has three levels (yellow, red and blue) and access to three streets. One may enter from 7 a.m. to 1 a.m. and leave at any time of the day or night. Vertical post lighting increases shoppers' perception of safety while aesthetic materials such as granite, cobblestone and wrought-iron railings make the garage a more attractive setting. Shoppers coming to or from the garage pass through spacious walkways with a glass canopy nearly 100 feet overhead. One end of the walkway opens onto a large wall of vegetation. With a view to meeting public

concerns, there are parking spaces with recharge terminals for electric vehicles and round-the-clock surveillance through 69 video cameras linked to a security center.

The project had 18 months for construction, timed to the 24-month period for the redevelopment zone as a whole. Traffic at the site was constrained during construction to avoid disruption of local residents.

A number of name retailers chose Les Passages de l'Hôtel de Ville as their first shopping center presence, including Alain Figaret, Balthazar, Cyrillus, Gerry Weber, Les Petites, Mexx and others. Retail categories represented among the stores include fashion, gifts and leisure, eateries, home goods, services and personal care.

Parking areas are color-coded to ease identification by shoppers.

Designers chose glass, metal and stone as finishing materials to create unity with adjacent buildings. A vegetation wall enhances the visual appeal of a landing between two escalators between the garage and the mall.

Madrid Xanadú

Arroyomolinos, Madrid, Spain

Owner and Management Company:
Madrid Xanadú 2003 S.L.
Arroyomolinos, Madrid, Spain

Development and Leasing Company:
The Mills Corporation
Arlington, Virginia, United States

Design and Production Architect:
Chapman Taylor España
Madrid, Spain

Graphic Design:
Kiku Obata
St. Louis, Missouri, United States
and
Communication Arts
Boulder, Colorado, United States

Lighting Designer:
Bliss Fasman, Inc.
New York, New York, United States

Landscape Architect:
MESA
Dallas, Texas, United States
and
Susana Canogar Paisajismo
Madrid, Spain

Gross size of center:
1,706,252 sq. ft.

**Gross leasable area
(shop space, excluding anchors, ECI and
Snow Dome):**
776,153 sq. ft.

Type of center:
Tourist destination center

Physical description:
Enclosed mall

Location of trading area:
Suburban

Population:
- Primary trading area
  736,982

- Secondary trading area
  4,260,738

Development schedule
- Original opening date
  May 16, 2003

Parking spaces:
- Present number
  7,349

*L*ike Kublai Khan's famed Xanadú, the city of earthly delights, Madrid Xanadú is a place to enjoy one's free time. The building plan has two sections — the retail center and the leisure center.

Shoppers come into the retail center through four entries: Puerta de la Amatista, Puerta de la Esmeralda, Puerta de la Perla and Puerta de Oro — respectively the "doors" of amethyst, emerald, pearl and gold — each named for the ornamental structures that fill the windows of each entry. The two-level retail section is an orchestrated composition of international art and fashion forms, textures, decoration, patterns, colors, lights and movement inspired by the regional Spanish imagery.

There are two retail shopping streets, El Paseo and La Gallaria, both light-filled spaces with vaulted ceilings and bridges spanning the openings between floors. The streets are intersected by three plazas — one for fashion, one that transitions to the leisure center

An 800-foot indoor ski slope (right) is the major entertainment attraction among many others at Madrid Xanadú.

and a central plaza decorated with murals and custom chandeliers. The fashion district includes sculptures by two internationally known Spanish artists. Nearly three-fourths of retailers are apparel stores. There is also a hypermarket.

Artists and craftspeople from throughout Europe and the United States created many of the design elements. Murals are by French and Spanish illustrators, furniture is from Italy and Spain, chandeliers and light fixtures from Spain and Germany, terrazzo flooring from Portugal and other design

MAJOR TENANTS		
NAME	TYPE	GLA (SQ. FT.)
Snow Dome	Indoor slope	245,072
El Corte Inglés Sport	Retail	15,037
Zara	Apparel	21,926
H&M	Apparel	31,194
Nike	Apparel	6,307
Benetton	Apparel	12,658

Strong design elements (below) accent both interiors and landscaped areas.

features from Spain, Italy, Portugal and the United States.

The leisure center is designed for the entire family. It is open until 2 a.m. on weeknights and 4 a.m. on weekends. Focused on a large, two-level elliptical space, the leisure center is ringed with restaurants, bars, cafés and a variety of entertainment experiences, including race-carting, movies, nightclubs, bowling, carnival rides and music. The translucent fabric roof brings the Spanish sunlight to the colorful patterned terrazzo floor.

The lower level of the leisure area contains La Arboleda, where more than 800 customers can dine under groves of olive trees and watch activity at Xanadú's Parque de Nieve, an 800-foot downhill slope that offers a year-round alpine-skiing experience. The leisure area's upper level is La Terrazza, where shoppers can dine on interior and exterior restaurant terraces or sit on balconies and bridges and view activity below. A tree-inspired canopy branches over the balconies. Two large, rotating graphic disks and two projection screens offer visual messages. At night, the translucent roof becomes a theatrically lit "night sky."

Successfully combining retail and entertainment has made Madrid Xanadú a destination for tourists and locals alike.

A translucent fabric roof (above and right) allows natural light to bathe the expansive mall area.

Below, the ski slope (at left) makes an indelible impression on shoppers approaching Madrid Xanadú.

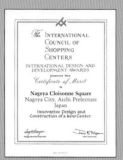

Nagoya Cloisonne Square

Nagoya City, Aichi Prefecture, Japan

Owner:
Tanyou Shoukai General Partnership
Nagoya City, Aichi Prefecture, Japan

Management Company:
Ando Cloisonne Co., Ltd.
Nagoya City, Aichi Prefecture, Japan

Design/Production/Landscape Architect:
Takenaka Corporation (Building Design Department)
Tokyo, Japan

Graphic Design:
Kyong-Hee Cho (Studio OP)
Tokyo, Japan

Lighting Designer:
Yamagiwa Corp. DFA
Tokyo, Japan

General Contractor:
Takenaka Corporation
Tokyo, Japan

Development and Leasing Company:
Takenaka Corporation (Office of Business Development)
Tokyo, Japan

Gross size of center:
14,556 sq. ft.

**Gross leasable area
(small shop space, excluding anchors):**
9,607 sq. ft.

Total acreage of site:
.34 acres

Type of center:
Fashion/specialty center

Physical description:
Free-standing two-level center

Location of trade area:
Urban Central Business District

Population:
- Primary trading area
  1,540,000

- Secondary trading area
  3,380,000

- Annualized percentage of shoppers
  anticipated to be from outside trade area
  10%

Development schedule:
- Original opening date
  October 5, 2002

It has long been an unwritten rule of development in Japan to use the maximum allowable floor-to-area ratio (FAR), but the creators of Nagoya Cloisonne Square in Nagoya, Japan's fourth-largest city, instead chose to design a boutique retail facility on two floors, using only one-eighth of the permissible FAR.

The owner has operated a cloisonne store at this site for over 120 years. In recent years, luxury-brand retailers have opened free-standing flagship stores on Otsu Street, to which the owner's recessed property has two access points. With the renewed retail interest in the area, the owner — who had planned to renovate merely the cloisonne store — chose to renovate the entire site. Earlier, it had comprised one shop, two offices, a storage area, a residence and a warehouse. The new plan has the new cloisonne shop, a cloisonne museum, an Italian fashion retailer and a renowned Italian café in its first location outside Italy.

Nagoya Cloisonne Square in Japan has only two entrances from the street, so they were made particularly appealing.

In the center of the site is a courtyard surrounded by the fashion store, café and cloisonne store, giving much-needed open space and tranquility in the neighborhood. The courtyard takes up 35% of the site's area and is planted with green moss, a natural vegetation helpful in preventing the "heat-island" phenomenon common in urban developments.

The decision to lessen the FAR was both aesthetic and pragmatic. If the facility were small, it would be possible to avoid regulations that would have required parking spaces within the project. This allowed the developer to maximize the floor area for rent at the street level for greater profit.

The site is shaped like an irregular horseshoe, with only two small points of connection to the street. Several steps give the entries good impact on passersby. Large flagstone and cloisonne artwork decorate the passageway to the cloisonne store, which serves to draw in pedestrians. The fashion store's transparent white facade also beckons to passing shoppers. External walls at one entrance are made of a two-layered concrete board of a natural stone aggregate.

Extensive use of glass (above) unifies the various types of shops on the property. Cloisonne and Italian fashion (below) create an upscale image on this street full of luxury-brand names.

To remind visitors of the historic nature of the original shop on the site, traditional Japanese store lanterns and stones that had been in the garden before redevelopment were reused in the new scheme, which blends old and new in an interesting retail mix.

Café patrons can view the courtyard while museum goers view the historic cloisonne collection.

MAJOR TENANTS		
NAME	**TYPE**	**GLA (SQ. FT.)**
MaxMara Nagoya	Apparel	8,530
Ando Cloisonne Nagoya	Cloisonne shop	1,793
Shippu Club – Ando Collection	Museum/multipurpose space	1,278
Caffé Arti e Mestieri	Restaurant	1,067

The two-story fashion store (below) looks out onto the courtyard, which offers a tranquil island in downtown Nagoya.

Okinawa Outlet Mall Ashibinaa

Tomigusuku-shi, Okinawa Prefecture, Japan

Owner:
Daiwa Information Services Co., Ltd.
Tokyo, Tokyo, Japan

Management Company:
Tech.R&DS Co., Ltd.
Tokyo, Tokyo, Japan

Design Architect:
Laguarda, Low Architects LLC.
Dallas, Texas, United States

Production Architect:
Laguarda, Low + Tanamachi Architects Inc.
Tokyo, Tokyo, Japan
and
Shimizu Corporation Inc. Kyushu Branch
Fukuoka, Fukuoka Prefecture, Japan

Graphic Design:
Redmond Schwartz Mark Design
San Clemente, California, United States

Lighting Designer:
Bliss-Fasma Lighting Design
New York, New York, United States

Landscape Architect and General Contractor:
Shimizu Corporation Inc. Kyushu Branch
Fukuoka, Fukuoka Prefecture, Japan

Development Company:
Daiwa Information Services Co., Ltd.
Tokyo, Tokyo, Japan

Leasing Company:
Vende Valore Inc.
Tokyo, Tokyo, Japan

Gross size of center:
228,900 sq. ft.

**Gross leasable area
(small shop space, excluding anchors):**
148,136 sq. ft.

Total acreage of site:
11.6 acres

Type of center:
Outlet center

Physical description:
Open two-level mall

Location of trading area:
Suburban

Population:
- Primary trading area
  1,300,000
- Secondary trading area
  5,000,000
- Annualized percentage of shoppers
  anticipated to be from outside trade area
  80%

Development schedule:
- Original opening date
  December 15, 2002

Parking spaces:
- Present number
  2,000

*At Okinawa Outlet
Mall Ashibinaa, the
stores are grouped
in two areas (upper
right): a Vehicular
Loop (foreground)
and a Pedestrian
Loop (rear).*

Okinawa Outlet Mall Ashibinaa is a two-level outlet mall designed to attract local residents as well as visitors from mainland Japan and surrounding countries. It serves as the initial development tool and catalyst for the reclaiming of the Okinawa waterfront. Inspired by Okinawa's heritage as an island-state, the lot design creates spatial uses reminiscent of Greek agoras—formal plazas. There are three components.

The Pedestrian Loop is a retail area built on narrow, nonlinear streets. Its retail alleys are partially shaded by suspended canvasses, extended roof overhangs and arcades. Open spaces are positioned randomly to evoke discovery and shopper interest.

Another retail area, the Vehicular Loop, has a more traditional layout, including a strong axial organization. Here, motor vehicles mingle with pedestrians. Shoppers visiting only one store have the opportunity to park

directly in front of their destination — this function has increased mall visits, especially during weekdays. The mix of people and vehicles strengthens the center's image as an urban shopping district.

The third component is a formal plaza or Agora, sited at the intersection of the pedestrian and vehicular loops. Public and commercial events are held in the Agora and it has become a community gathering place. It has become so popular that on weekends, the adjacent Vehicular Loop is often converted to a purely pedestrian plaza for festivals and performances.

Tourists are attracted to the center for its upscale shopping choices.

Eleven tenants, including Gucci Group and Hugo Boss, have chosen Okinawa Outlet Mall Ashibinaa as their first outlet locations in Japan. There are about 65 shops, focused heavily on apparel, along with a number of food and beverage outlets locat-

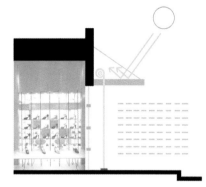

1. VINYL SCREEN ATTACHED TO THE COLUMN   2. VINYL SCREEN ATTACHED TO THE CANOPY

In a promenade (top), awnings and canopies shield shoppers from the bright Okinawa sunlight. There are 65 stores (lower left) focused heavily on apparel.

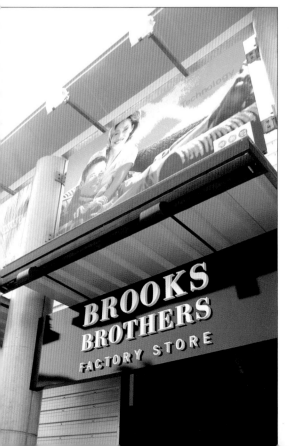

MAJOR TENANTS

NAME	TYPE	GLA (SQ. FT.)
Gucci/Yves Saint Laurent	Apparel	9,326
Brooks Brothers	Apparel	6,332
Next Door	——	4,861
ABC Mart	——	4,665
Adidas	Footwear	4,485
Fine7	——	4,430
New Yorker	——	4,261

ed in a well-shaded food court above the Vehicular Loop stores.

Design builds on shades of gray and brick. While it is an open-air project, canopies at the second-story level provide shade and relief from the tropical Okinawa sunshine. Exterior facades are kept simple, as in many outlet malls. Plain concrete two-story columns throughout the project evoke the columns of the ancient Greek design that inspired the lot plan.

The developers and designers decided to position the mall as an urban marketplace, which is why parking and vehicular circulation were introduced into the center of the project. The project was a purely private venture, but because of its status as the first project in the reclaimed-land master plan, local officials took special interest in it. After seeing its success, they may use it as an example for future development.

The Agora (left) — a formal plaza — has become a popular community gathering place.

In the food court (top) and a retail area (above), design was kept simple as befitting an outlet mall.

Plaza Mayor

Málaga, Spain

**Owner and Management Company,
Design and Production Architect,
Graphic Designer and
Development and Leasing Company:**
Sonae Sierra
Lisbon, Portugal

Gross size of center:
359,040 sq. ft.

**Gross leasable area
(small shop space, excluding anchors):**
163,299 sq. ft.

Type of center:
Regional fashion/leisure center

Physical description:
Open mall

Location of trading area:
Suburban

Population:
- Primary trading area
  658,000
- Secondary trading area
  882,000
- Annualized percentage of shoppers
  anticipated to be from outside trade area
  10%

Development schedule:
- Original opening date
  April 19, 2002

Parking spaces:
- Present number
  2,350

*Shoppers
approaching Plaza
Mayor see what
looks like a typical
Andalusian village,
with streets,
cupolas, plazas and
two-story homes.*

*P*laza Mayor, on Spain's southern Costa del Sol not far from the city of Málaga, is a leisure center designed for locals and tourists taking a break from the area's renowned golf courses. In addition to 30 retail shops, the open-air center has the 20-screen Yelmo Cineplex with 4,900 seats, a health club, a family entertainment center with a 20-lane bowling alley and a discotheque. There is also a child day-care center.

MAJOR TENANTS		
NAME	**TYPE**	**GLA (SQ. FT.)**
Yelmo Cineplex	Multiplex cinemas	84,077
Solinca Health Club	Fitness	45,973
Big Fun Center	Recreation	38,341
Nike Factory Store	Footwear	15,080
Pacha Disco	Nightclub	12,270

The mall area suggests the local architecture, both in design and materials used.

There are four plazas and a street. Traditional Andalusian cuisine can be found at the Plaza del Azahar. Fast food, the cinemas and Spain's largest video wall are at the center's core area, also called Plaza Mayor. Plaza del Agua offers an interactive fountain on which visitors can create their own water show. Plaza Brava provides bars and entertainment. Finally, Zoco Street has 30 shops focused on fashion.

Andalusia's traditional architecture inspired the design of Plaza Mayor. As shoppers approach, they see what looks like a typical village of two-story houses with chimneys and home-style windows. The colors of the "houses" range from pastels to bold primary hues. A few cupolas suggest town centers.

Inside, shoppers find further evidence of village-style design — there are streets, squares, facades, roofs, green areas and fountains. Design materials include stone, ceramic pavements, aged tiles, wood and iron — all found in abundance in the surrounding community as well. There is a "green area" of over 215,000 square feet where the developer planted over 1,000 new trees.

There are nine water features. One is a gigantic flowerpot, another is synchronized with a tower clock. There are Arabic-style water channels to hydrate orange trees at the Plaza del

Azahar. All fountain water is treated so it is always clean, and the mall's facades contain a vaporized water system so shoppers can feel the fresh humidified water as they walk through the mall.

The mall's leisure focus called for new technology, including a state-of-the-art hi-fi system capable of creating distinct musical environments in each of the mall's 11 zones. Liquid crystal screens even provide entertainment for those using the restrooms. Plaza Mayor also has a computerized visitor counting system to support marketing and leasing plans.

The developer reports higher-than-expected performance for the center. The average of 3.6 million people each month demonstrates that Plaza Mayor has become a major leisure and retail destination.

Water features and art contribute to the leisure focus of Plaza Mayor.

San Marino Shopping Center

Guayaquil, Guayas, Ecuador

Owner and Management Company:
Inmobiliaria Nuevo Mundo S. A.
Guayaquil, Guayas, Ecuador

Design Architect and Graphic Designer:
Development Design Group, Inc.
Baltimore, Maryland, United States

Production Architect/Lighting Designer/Landscape Architect:
Michel Deller Aquitectos
Quito, Ecuador

General Contractor:
Constructora Ekron
Quito, Ecuador

Development Company:
Urbanizadora Naciones Unidas S. A.
Guayaquil, Guayas, Ecuador

Leasing Company:
Inmobiliaria Nuevo Mundo S. A.
Guayaquil, Guayas, Ecuador

Gross size of center:
756,000 sq. ft.

Gross leasable area (small shop space, excluding anchors):
283,000 sq. ft.

Total acreage of site:
4.1 acres

Type of center:
Fashion/lifestyle center

Physical description:
Enclosed mall with streetfront retail

Location of trading area:
Urban but not downtown

Population:
- Primary trading area
  800,000

- Secondary trading area
  340,000

- Annualized percentage of shoppers anticipated to be from outside trade area
  8%-10%

Development schedule:
- Original opening date
  June 26, 2003

Parking spaces:
- Present number
  1,298

San Marino Shopping Center offers street-level retail to the residents and tourists of Guayaquil, Ecuador.

*S*an Marino Shopping Center in Guayaquil, Ecuador, is a retail and entertainment complex that capitalized on local artisans in applying the "look" of historic Spanish colonial architecture to a modern mall.

The mall links to the community in the most direct way – street-level retail, with its bold graphics and vibrant lighting effects, eye-catching facades and inviting architectural elements. An iconic bell and clock tower rises 110 feet above the street, giving San Marino a public face. Towers and cupolas lend regional flavor to the design, as do clay roof tiles and stuccoed, plaster-finished walls. Intricate ironwork is inspired by the work of Alexandre-Gustave Eiffel.

Many of the materials in the center were crafted on-site. Local artists hand-carved much of the center's concrete and cast much of the detailed handrails. The skilled labor force used "old school" con-

MAJOR TENANTS		
NAME	TYPE	GLA (SQ. FT.)
Supercines	Multiplex cinema	33,023
DePrati Hogar	Home furnishings	16,471
Etafashion	Apparel	12,822
DePrati Niños Y Zona Junior	Apparel	10,811
Pycca	Home furnishings	10,988

The main hall at San Marino (left and above left) hosted 800,000 visitors its first year.

struction techniques, which lent innate identity to the building's design. The city's existing architectural elements laid the pattern for the details shown in cast-iron lamps, posts, kiosks, wrought-iron railings, hand-painted mosaic tiles and reproductions of traditional marble and stonework.

Despite embracing Old World design, San Marino is technologically modern, including an advanced surveillance system. An alarm system monitors every area of the complex, and panic alarms can be found throughout the mall.

The tenant list is oriented toward apparel, with about 60 stores offering clothing for men, women and children, about a dozen shoe stores and another dozen stores focused on jewelry and eyewear. Home design accounts for another 15 units. There are about a dozen service establishments and about three dozen food stores, including restaurants, food court tenants

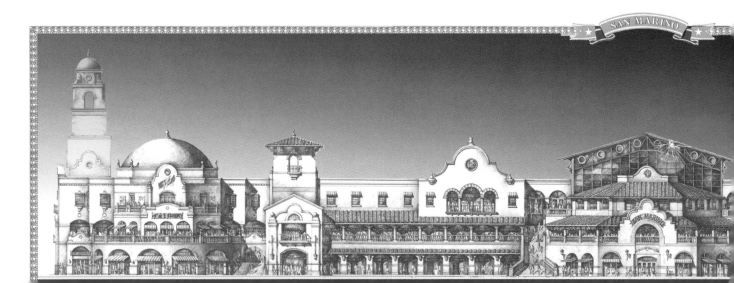

and food specialty stores. Entertainment attractions include a 10-screen multiplex cinema, bowling alleys and a play zone.

There are three shopping levels, with potential for four stores to expand upwards onto a fourth — mezzanine — level. Kiosks have a strong presence on the middle shopping level.

Through its attentiveness to design found in the neighboring community, the center maintains the easy ambience of a hillside village while capturing the energy and romantic flair of a Latin American market. By combining an enclosed galleria with surrounding outdoor elements, San Marino Shopping Center achieves its retail and entertainment goals.

Architecture of the surrounding community informed the design choices at San Marino.

Canberra Centre

Canberra, ACT, Australia

Owner and Management Company:
QIC Real Estate
Brisbane, Queensland, Australia

Design and Production Architect:
Daryl Jackson Alastair Swayn Pty Ltd
Canberra, ACT, Australia

Graphic Design:
Swell Design & Daryl Jackson Alastair Swayn Pty Ltd
Canberra, ACT, Australia

Lighting Designer:
GHD Pty Ltd & Daryl Jackson Alastair Swayn Pty Ltd
Canberra, ACT, Australia

Landscape Architect:
JEA (John Easthope & Associates) &
Daryl Jackson Alastair Swayn Pty Ltd
Canberra, ACT, Australia

General Contractor:
Bovis Lend Lease Pty Limited
Canberra, ACT, Australia

Development and Leasing Company:
QIC Real Estate
Brisbane, Queensland, Australia

Gross size of center:
613,758 sq. ft.

Amount of space renovated:
613,758 sq. ft.

Gross leasable area
(small shop space, excluding anchors):
222,350 sq. ft.

Total acreage of site:
13.4 acres

Type of center:
Regional center

Physical description:
Open and enclosed mall

Location of trading area:
Urban Central Business District

Population:
- Primary trading area
  270,612

- Secondary trading area
  246,774

- Annualized percentage of shoppers
  anticipated to be from outside trade area
  8.1%

Development schedule:
- Original opening date
  March 26, 1963

- Current expansion date
  November 11, 2002

Parking spaces:
- Present number
  3,300

The Canberra Centre Consolidation Project in Australia's capital stretched over six years and required extensive consultation with the public and government units. Here, the forecourt provides access to a new shopping arcade.

The Canberra Centre Consolidation Project sought to reassert the center as the major shopping destination in the Australian Capital Territory. Prior to development, Canberra Centre stretched over three disconnected city blocks. One block held core retail stores and offices, one block contained a supermarket and parking decks and the last had a Target discount department store and more deck parking. Market research prior to redevelopment also found gaps in the center's tenant mix – most notably high-end fashion and lifestyle retailers. The research also unearthed shoppers' safety concerns about the presence of city streets within the retail space and their perception that the center did not have an easily recognizable "place to meet."

The developer's ability to purchase one of the city streets from the government was the crucial element in the project's evolution, plus subsequent persuasion of

Photograph: Gollings

Photograph: CCM

MAJOR TENANTS		
NAME	**TYPE**	**GLA (SQ. FT.)**
Myer	Department store	145,444
David Jones	Department store	131,179
Target	Discount department store	75,139
Supabarn City Market	Supermarket	27,771
Lincraft	Homewares	11,840

Photograph: DJAS

Consolidation included merging buildings stretched over three city blocks into one seamless entity. In the aerial view, the mall is the large structure in the upper right. The forecourt (right) reclaims public space for a gathering place.

Photograph: Gollings

planning authorities to allow the central business district street to be closed and converted to a three-block retail mall. Purchase negotiations, zoning changes and development stretched over six years. Design work commenced in 1997, and the developer bought the street in 1999. Construction began in 2001 and took 18 months to complete. Overall, the project cost $40 million (US).

After extensive consultation with the public and government, the developer built a two-story arcade along one of the streets that divided the old center, turning the old roadway into a pedestrian walkway yet preserving it as part of the perceived public realm. About 40 specialty stores opened in the new arcade and in an extended indoor first-floor galleria. Upgrading and refurbishment of adjacent retail areas created a seamless flow from the arcade.

The current center also expanded its upper level, crossing over a public road and connecting to the other blocks. In all, the consolida-tion resulted in the reorientation and refurbishment of the Target store, a new retail bridge over an existing street, the reclaimed pedestrian street through the arcade, a new public forecourt, the new galleria, renovation of the parking decks, a bridge connecting the office unit to the parking area and refurbishment of the existing common area.

The center and street retail stores remained open for business. Coordinating the project around shopping hours took major effort.

Photograph: Trends

The mall area (left) looks cleaner and more sophisticated after the renovation (above).

Photograph: CCM

Photograph: DJAS

The new food court (right) features a brighter look, with new furniture, as compared to the old food court (left). Abundant natural light (below) reduces the need for artificial illumination during the day.

Photograph: Trends

Photograph: Gollings

Much of the construction took place at night and was scheduled to stretch over only one holiday shopping season.

Within the center, specialized hoardings shielded construction from public view. The hoardings also contained graphics to inform shoppers about the renovation and expansion, including the introduction of new stores. Temporary bridges were constructed to maintain the links between stores and parking.

Shoppers received parking discounts nearby, designed to limit disruption to the center's traffic flow. Courtesy crews answered customers' questions and helped them find relocated stores. New directional signage was installed. New safety measures included 24-hour security.

Published communication took many forms. Retailers attended information sessions prior to, during and after construction. Management worked directly with individual tenants. Territory residents received a total of 70,000 flyers that outlined project timing and road closures. Double-page newspaper ads reinforced the information.

Refurbishment of the existing

Photograph: Trends

A new ground-floor arcade (left) has replaced a city street. Black and white is the color scheme for new signage (above) and the center's new logo.

Photograph: Gollings

Photograph: DJAS

Photograph: Gollings

Photograph: Gollings

Exterior views hint at the complexity of unifying a multi-level mall sprawling over three city blocks.

Photograph: Gollings

mall took place for its own sake and to create a seamless "look" with the new section. Common areas were repainted. Both sections would use the same balustrade treatments, lighting and furniture. Renovated areas included restrooms, key retailers' storefronts and the food court. New fixtures provided a uniform level of artificial lighting. A new switching system allows greater control of lighting and cost efficiencies. Inside and out, 100 closed-circuit monitors attend to safety concerns, which are addressed by on-site security 24 hours per day, seven days per week.

The consolidation required a new logo for the center, since the old logo showed four squares symbolizing the city streets running through the center. The old color scheme based on local heritage made way for a new white-on-black design with a clean modern font reflective of the center's award-winning architecture.

Good planning and communication allowed the center to achieve a 1.2% sales growth even during consolidation. Post-renovation saw sales growth of 24% and traffic growth of nearly 15%, confirming the value of the project for developer and shoppers alike.

Photograph: DJAS

Photograph: DJAS

Stairwells, elevator lobbies, parking lots and mall areas are all scanned by a total of 100 video cameras, which in turn are monitored by security personnel every day, around the clock.

Photograph: Trends

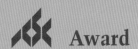
Dadeland Mall

Miami, Florida, United States

Owner and Management Companies:

Simon Property Group
Indianapolis, Indiana, United States
and

Morgan Stanley's Prime Property Fund
Atlanta, Georgia, United States

Design Architect:

Thompson, Ventulett, Stainback & Associates
Atlanta, Georgia, United States

Production Architect:

Johnson Associates Architects
Miami, Florida, United States

Graphic Design:

Lorenc Yoo Design
Atlanta, Georgia, United States

Lighting Designer:

The Lighting Practice
Philadelphia, Pennsylvania, United States

Landscape Architect:

Whitkin Design Group
Miami, Florida, United States

General Contractor:

DPMI
Youngstown, Ohio, United States

Development and Leasing Company:

Simon Property Group
Indianapolis, Indiana, United States

Gross size of center:
1,310,000 sq. ft.

Amount of space renovated:
1,310,000 sq. ft.

**Gross leasable area
(small shop space, excluding anchors):**
1,142,000 sq. ft.

Total acreage of site:
70 acres

Type of center:
Regional center

Physical description:
Enclosed mall

Location of trading area:
Suburban

Population:
* Primary trading area
  300,000

* Secondary trading area
  1,100,000

* Annualized percentage of shoppers
  anticipated to be from outside trade area
  54%

Development schedule:
* Original opening date
  1962

* Current expansion date
  April 2003

Parking spaces:
* Present number
  6,879

* 300 parking spaces added in renovation

The design of the new entry "jewel box" built geometry, scale and lighting into an icon for Dadeland Mall in Miami, Florida.

Built in 1962 as an open-air center, Dadeland Mall in Miami, Florida, had since been enclosed and expanded several times. While it remained a successful property and popular among both locals and tourists from many nations, the multiple expansions had created a complicated layout with long, narrow concourses using dissimilar finishes. Meanwhile, the Miami market had become increasingly competitive, causing Dadeland Mall's owners to think about reinventing the 40-year-old mall.

Beyond the dull look and unorthodox layout, the mall lacked amenities sought by wealthier shoppers. The owners hoped that a complete renovation, better traffic flow and more extras would attract new upscale tenants.

Overall, the design team wanted to express both the luxurious tropical-resort environment and

the edgy sophistication that defines Miami. Forms and colors were inspired by the clean geometries of South Beach, the lush terrain, the soft beach colors and the sun, shadow and glamour of Miami. Designers focused on four aspects: the main entrance exterior, the entrance lobby, the food court and concourses and mall courts.

All the mall entrances lacked scale, image and identity. There was no identifiable "main entrance" that could be seen from the road and serve as an icon for the center. Renovation created a "jewel box" entrance clearly visible from the street. An expansive plaza, a valet porte cochere and an active fountain further enhanced the main entrance.

The entrance lobby, which sits within the "jewel," is a welcoming and gathering space where shoppers can meet, wait for

The old center court space (below) was dark and complicated traffic flow. The new space (right) lets in plenty of natural light and clears the view of nearby stores.

MAJOR TENANTS		
NAME	**TYPE**	**GLA (SQ. FT.)**
Macy's	Department store	421, 073
Macy's Home Gallery	Department store	210, 000
Saks Fifth Avenue	Department store	78, 669
Limited/Express	Apparel	80, 000
Nordstrom	Department store	150, 090
JCPenney	Department store	170, 896

The old west concourse and storefronts (smaller photos) made way for modern design, incorporating new ceiling forms, a light color palette and many detailing enhancements.

restaurant seats or relax. A glass vaulted ceiling rises 40 feet, allowing daytime shadows to wash softly over the space. At night, the space is dramatically illuminated by a sculptural chandelier and artistic backlit glass panels.

The old food court inhabited the space of a former grocery store – dark and dismal, with no character of its own. Low ceilings and built-ins divided the space and reinforced the closed-in feeling. The new food court serves as an oasis in the renovated mall. The roof over the seating area was raised. New and amusing graphics include geckos embossed on columns. Backlit art glass and custom-designed tabletops contribute to the food court's enhanced identity.

Existing concourses were dark, dated and heavy. Natural light was limited and resulted in uncomfortable glare. The east and west concourses had different

The old arrival lobby (right) was undistinguished at best. The new lobby (above) suggests the resort ambience of the surrounding city.

paths and provided no help in unifying the disjointed floor plan. Without affecting the existing structure, the developers rebuilt the entire mall interior, relying on smooth curves and a soft color palette that both maximizes and softens the natural light. Floor and ceiling patterns now reflect each other and the look of existing columns. Elegant finishes in soft neutral palettes clad the modern forms. Marble floors and details such as embossed tapered columns, dichroic glass and integrated signage add to visual interest and shopper satisfaction.

Bright, distinctive graphics welcome shoppers to Dadeland Mall.

Soft seating areas are just one of the improvements (below) in the renovated east concourse (an old concourse is pictured on the right).

According to the center's marketing studies, Dadeland shoppers — including tourists — tended to be fashion-conscious, prompting the mall to seek appropriate retailers. To upgrade the mix, the mall added a Nordstrom anchor and units such as Movado, Oakley and CocoParis. The Hispanic and international clientele also sees shopping as a social occasion to be enjoyed in large groups with friends and family. To satisfy those shoppers and lengthen their visits, the mall offered them new services such as valet parking and bag service, as well as new amenities such as large soft seating areas, updated restrooms and the food court enhancements.

The mall renovations inspired similar work by all the existing anchor stores, contributing to the totally new look of this popular Miami shopping destination.

Renovations extended to every mall entry (top of page). The new food court (left) has its own exciting identity, erasing memories of the old food court (above left), housed in a former supermarket space.

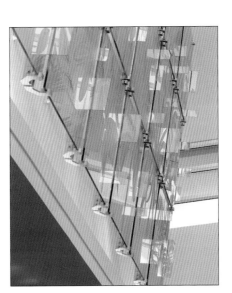

Whether it's custom-designed tabletops, glass walls, etched glass or geckos on columns, the new look of Dadeland Mall is attracting upscale retailers and upscale shoppers alike.

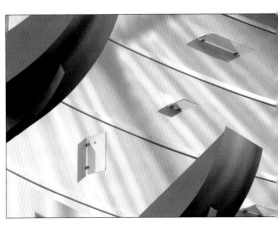

Charlottesville Fashion Square
Charlottesville, Virginia, United States

Owners and Management Company:
Simon Property Group, Inc.
Indianapolis, Indiana, United States

Design Architect:
Cooper Carry, Inc.
Atlanta, Georgia, United States

Production Architect:
EJD & Associates Company
Youngstown, Ohio, United States

Graphic Designer:
Lorenc+Yoo Design
Roswell, Georgia, United States

Lighting Designer:
Carrie Walker
Atlanta, Georgia, United States

General Contractor:
DPMI
Youngstown, Ohio, United States

Development and Leasing Company:
Simon Property Group, Inc.
Indianapolis, Indiana, United States

Gross size of center:
571,980 sq. ft.

Amount of space renovated:
571,980 sq. ft.

**Gross leasable area
(small shop space, excluding anchors):**
190,827 sq. ft.

Total acreage of site:
60 acres

Type of center:
Regional center

Physical description:
Enclosed mall

Location of trading area:
Middle market

Population:
- Primary trading area
  93,578

- Secondary trading area
  50,388

- Annualized percentage of shoppers
  anticipated to be from outside trade area
  0.4%

Development schedule:
- Original opening date
  March 1980

- Current expansion date
  November 2002

Parking spaces:
- Present number
  3,289

- No parking spaces added in renovation

*C*harlottesville Fashion Square opened in 1980 as the dominant retail development in the historic region of Virginia. Since then, new retail centers had opened nearby and in Richmond, Virginia, and Washington, DC, giving customers more options for fashion shopping, albeit at a significant distance. Customers' perceptions were that Charlottesville Fashion Square was adequate for basic shopping needs, but no longer the environment for stylish apparel.

The mall had not received a significant update since its construction and had major deficiencies. Customers could not see the entrances from the parking areas. Graphics and the mall logo were dated and ineffective. An existing terrazzo floor was in serious disrepair. A built-in planter and seating areas inhibited cross-mall shopping and disrupted pedestrian movement. A series of very small skylights were not energy-efficient and their haphazard pattern created a confusing ceiling

The new octagonal main entrance at Charlottesville Fashion Square (above) has architectural power. The former entrance (top) was utilitarian at best.

MAJOR TENANTS

NAME	TYPE	GLA (SQ. FT.)
Belk	Department stores (2)	181,155
Sears	Department store	103,946
JCPenney	Department store	86,052

arrangement. Finally, mercury-vapor interior lighting lacked crispness and failed to give adequate levels of light and renditions of color.

To meet the shoppers' need for fashion retailers, the tenant mix required upgrading. Surveys showed that the three most desirable small shop tenants would be Eddie Bauer, J. Crew and Abercrombie & Fitch.

Eddie Bauer (left bottom) was one of several new retailers included in the new tenant mix to draw upscale shoppers. The pylons (top) show the dramatic impact of the new logo design.

Steps and sharp corners complicated traffic flow at the prerenovated mall areas (left center). The new mall (above) softens the angles and adds planters.

The modest renovation budget allowed only cosmetic changes. The center now has a new logo, integrated into the mall entrances, which in turn have been demarcated with simple architectural forms embedded in the building. These structures glow with light, presenting patrons with a clear identity for the mall and setting expectations for the new interior look. New porcelain tile flooring has been arranged in classical patterns that differentiate the areas within the mall.

Key courts benefit from natural illumination from larger skylights. A new artificial-lighting program includes both classical pendant fixtures and others mounted to surfaces that produce light "textures" on the ceiling at night.

Past design (top center and left center) was stark; oddly placed skylights complicated ceiling patterns. Now, soft seating areas (top left) and twinned columns (top right) create a human scale. At center court (bottom left), curved ribs create the illusion of a domed ceiling.

Center Court received special attention. Oddly placed single columns grew twins to create symmetry. The paired columns were clad in stone bases and mahogany-stained cherrywood that soar to the ceiling and match furniture. Curving semicircular ribs radiate outward from the center of a ceiling fixture to create the appearance of an interior dome.

The new tenant mix included all the stores identified in research, plus others, increasing visitors per month by 25% and confirming a successful renovation at Charlottesville Fashion Square.

Emmen Center

Emmenbrücke, Switzerland

Owner and Management Company:
Maus Frères SA
Geneva, Switzerland

Design and Landscape Architect:
Haskoll
London, England

Production Architect:
Interplan Projekt GmbH
Lucerne, Switzerland

Graphic Design:
DAP: Daly Albisser Partner GmbH
Lucerne, Switzerland

Lighting Designer:
Haskoll
London, England
and
Mottier SA/BS Elektro Engineering AG
Lucerne, Switzerland

General Contractor:
ARGE Shopping Centre c/o Anliker AG
Lucerne, Switzerland

Development and Leasing Company:
Maus Frères SA
Geneva, Switzerland

Gross size of center:
457,470 sq. ft.

Amount of space renovated:
457,470 sq. ft.

**Gross leasable area
(small shop space, excluding anchors):**
457,470 sq. ft.

Type of center:
Regional center

Physical description:
Enclosed mall

Location of trading area:
Urban but not Central Business District

Population:
• Primary trading area
  20,000

• Secondary trading area
  700,000

• Annualized percentage of shoppers
  anticipated to be from outside trade area
  4%

Development schedule:
• Original opening date
  1975

• Current expansion date
  September 2001

Parking spaces:
• Present number
  2,400

Switzerland's Emmen Center was improved inside and out and included a new tenant totem (opposite page, above) and new lighting design (opposite page, right). New retail space was added (opposite page, upper right) throughout the mall.

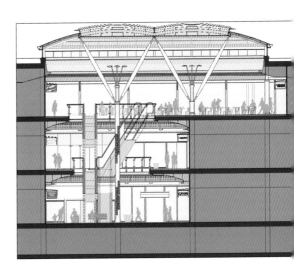

Built in 1975, Emmen Center in the Swiss town of Emmenbrücke was the largest shopping mall in the country. The developer decided to renovate and enlarge the center to increase its retail capacity, to stimulate interest from new retailers and to recapture the more sophisticated clientele in the trade area that had been lost to newer developments.

Before the renovation, Emmen Center consisted of a two-level shopping mall anchored by a department store and a supermar-

one into the department store anchor.

Inside, most illumination came from artificial lighting, despite the presence of small skylights. Finishes were dark and dated. A large part of the mall space was taken by a staircase between the two mall levels. Outside, the concrete-clad panels wrapping the center gave poor retail presence to passersby. The center seemed to have an introspective appearance with little tie-in to the surrounding neighborhood.

ket. There were about 60 small shops occupied by Swiss national and local retailers. There were several eateries, most notably the Manora restaurant at ground level, overlooking a gas station. Parking was located under the mall, on the roof and in a multi-story garage adjacent to the center. Most access to the shopping levels came via the car lots, although there were two dark and unwelcoming street entrances,

MAJOR TENANTS		
NAME	**TYPE**	**GLA (SQ. FT.)**
Manor	Department store	100,000
Manor	Supermarket	35,000
Vogele	Apparel	23,000
H & M	Apparel	20,000
Manora	Restaurant	10,750

The renewal strategy addressed all these concerns. Adding a second-floor mall at roof level created new retail space. The department store anchor was remodeled so it traded on three levels, releasing retail space on the lower two floors. The Manora restaurant was relocated, freeing up ground-floor space. The supermarket was extended, releasing even more ground-level footage.

The new Manora location was paired with other restaurants and cafés, creating a food focus on the mall's second floor. New elevators

Outside, concrete-clad panels (top) made way for a canopy and windows (center). Inside, new finishes improved storefronts, ceilings, handrails and floors.

Redesign of Emmen Center's exterior (left and left bottom) brought a contemporary look to the 30-year-old mall. The unrenovated center is pictured at top left.

Inside Emmen Center (above), a massive skylight is supported by structural "trees" that add visual interest at the highest levels.

and escalators aided vertical circulation. Graphic complements included a new mall logo and better external signage, which provided visible identity for the mall's retailers.

Internal finishes got special attention. New ceramic floor tiles were placed over existing conglomerate, saving time and expense and giving a consistent look to all three floors. Modeled ceilings incorporated perforated timber panels. Glass- and steel-post balustrades with timber handrails replaced the old void-edge balustrades.

New light fixtures improved illumination of the floors and the new ceiling treatments. Some of the fixtures pushed light through the openings in the mall floors, which were enlarged to ease pedestrian flow and improve

sightlines between the mall levels. A perforated metal bull-nose, introduced to form the junction with the ceiling, also contained a public-address system and a flexible lighting track that could be changed to satisfy staging needs of events and promotions. The new second-floor mall got a new glazed skylight, which was supported by structural "trees."

Outside, new cladding hid the old concrete panels. Bridge links from the multistory garage were relit and enclosed. Two new street-level entries were built, the department store entrance relocated and a canopy installed. A new tenant totem sign is mounted onto the canopy, giving the center new linkage to the surrounding city streets.

Le Carrefour Laval

Laval, Québec, Canada

Owner and Management Company:
Cadillac Fairview Corporation Limited
Toronto, Ontario, Canada

Designer:
Gervais Harding Associés
Montreal, Québec, Canada

Production Architect:
Groupe Archifin Inc
Montreal, Québec, Canada

Lighting Designer:
Gabriel/design
Ottawa, Ontario, Canada

Landscape Architect/Garden Court:
Rousseau Lefebvre
Laval, Québec, Canada

General Contractor:
C.A.L. Construction
Montreal, Québec, Canada

Development and Leasing Company:
Cadillac Fairview Corporation Limited
Toronto, Ontario, Canada

Gross size of center:
1,286,501 sq. ft.

Amount of space added:
306,150 sq. ft.

**Gross leasable area
(small shop space, excluding anchors):**
727,021 sq. ft.

Total acreage of site:
103 acres

Type of center:
Super-regional center

Physical description:
Enclosed mall

Location of trading area:
Suburban

Population:
- Primary trading area
  612,590

- Secondary trading area
  498,867

- Annualized percentage of shoppers
  anticipated to be from outside trade area
  26%

Development schedule:
- Original opening date
  August 1, 1974

- Current expansion date
  August 14, 2002

Parking spaces:
- Present number
  6,434

- 891 net parking spaces added in
  renovation

A major department store anchor had closed at Le Carrefour Laval shopping center in Québec, a 30-year-old mall. The successful mall had an extremely low vacancy rate, high sales performance and a waiting list of potential tenants. So, rather than just replace the anchor, the mall's developer chose also to add over 300,000 square feet of leasable space.

The expansion's anchor, La Maison Simons, was joined by large "name" stores like Zara,

the enticingly curved mall areas. Only real stone, metals and woods can be found among the expansion's finishes. Many services were enhanced, including parking, security, nursing rooms and washrooms, adding to the appeal for upscale shoppers.

The major focal point in the expansion is the Garden Court, with its plantings, fountains and café set in a town square atmosphere. Its decorative plantings are replaced seasonally and have

Sports Experts and Renaud-Bray Books. The new space also accommodated upscale retailers such as Tommy Hilfiger, La Cache, Mephisto, Swarovski, Godiva, Souris Mini and Chez Farfelu. The expansion space links to the older space through three promenades.

Visually, the design of the expansion matches the richness of the retailers in residence. French-styled "buildings" soar up to 30-feet high and suggest an urban enclosure. A café heightens the European ambience. Extra-high three-dimensional storefronts are carefully detailed. Clerestories and skylights wash daylight over

Le Carrefour Laval's new anchor, La Maison Simons (above), and mall entrances (above right) welcome shoppers. Inside (right), mosaic tile accents the Garden Court.

MAJOR TENANTS

NAME	TYPE	GLA (SQ. FT.)
La Baie	Department store	185,588
Sears	Department store	150,850
Rona L'Entrepôt	Home improvement	140,824
La Maison Simons	Department store	71,744

Both interiors (below) and exteriors (bottom) capitalize on long, gentle curves and plenty of glass to create design excitement.

Old mall areas (top and center) were drab and dated. The renovations (above) suggest a contemporary urban street scene.

New plantings, skylights and soft seating areas enhance all areas of the mall.

The Garden Court (above and right) has become a community gathering place at Le Carrefour Laval. Plantings change seasonally, including at Christmastime (right).

become a popular background for photographers. The Garden Court also serves, appropriately, as the site of an annual gala known as the "Bal des Fleurs," promoting the City of Laval's horticultural expertise.

Safety was a key goal throughout the 17-month expansion, in addition to maintaining customer and vehicular traffic. An adjacent free-standing cinema was demolished and an on-site winter snow dump was relocated to provide more parking. A new three-level parking structure was opened 10 months before the expansion's debut. All vehicular and pedestrian traffic signage was enhanced. Tenants supported a strict employee parking policy that reserved favorable parking for shoppers. There was a slight decrease in traffic during early construction, but no decline in sales.

The mall's enhancements were upgraded. A state-of-the-art security office uses video surveillance throughout the mall. Washroom facilities were doubled, family rooms were added for nursing and

child care and soft seating was installed. Designers replaced existing angled bulkheads to increase the sense of space and enable tenants to raise their storefronts.

Le Carrefour Laval's expansion was rapidly leased thanks to aggressive marketing, including production of a 3-D computer-generated "walk" through the expansion. The video premiered at a presentation to the entire retail community at a local hotel. Marketing focused on the positioning statement "Grandiose," used on outdoor billboards at strategic high-traffic intersections in primary and secondary markets. The center also used two television commercials, full-page newspaper ads and a preopening media tour.

The quality of the design in the expansion of Le Carrefour Laval has inspired tenants in the older part of the mall to spruce up their own stores and meet the new design standard.

Photographs: Wayne Lee
Top left and right photographs: Arsénio Corôa

Manhattan Village
Manhattan Beach, California, United States

Owner:
Madison Marquette
Washington, DC, United States

Management Company:
Madison Marquette
Los Angeles, California, United States

Design Architect:
Callison
Seattle, Washington, United States

Graphic Design:
Scott Architectural Graphics, Inc.
Santa Rosa, California, United States

Landscape Architect:
Mission Landscape
Santa Ana, California, United States

General Contractor:
J. M. Stitt Construction
Brea, California, United States

Development and Leasing Company:
Madison Marquette
Los Angeles, California, United States

Gross size of center:
505,000 sq. ft.

Amount of space renovated:
505,000 sq. ft.

Gross leasable area
(small shop space, excluding anchors):
100,000 sq. ft.

Total acreage of site:
45.2 acres

Type of center:
Regional center

Physical description:
Open-air and enclosed mall

Location of trading area:
Suburban

Population:
• Primary trading area
  220,000

• Secondary trading area
  426,000

• Annualized percentage of shoppers
  anticipated to be from outside trade area
  15%

Development schedule:
• Original opening date
  Early 1980s

• Current expansion date
  May 2003

Parking spaces:
• Present number
  2,405

A dated mall entrance (above right) is reclad in beach-like elements (right) at Manhattan Village in Southern California.

The 20-year-old Manhattan Village in Southern California was only 60% occupied and had a dated look when its owners chose to improve their investment and renovate the center. They adopted a two-phase plan: first, to upgrade the common areas and, next, to replace an existing building with two new ones. The new look sought to bring the Southern California ambience into the mall, thus creating a "village" that would enhance the mall's value to the community.

Phase I sought to remove dark and uninviting common areas. Updated entrances reflected the character of a village by the beach. The new design has larger doors and windows, as well as wood-louvered awnings and trel-lises. The dark food court was eliminated to make room for more tenant lease space. A new food focus was placed at Center Court, designed as a light and airy "beach house" using a large clerestory skylight, ceiling fans and a beached-wood ceiling and

MAJOR TENANTS

NAME	TYPE	GLA (SQ. FT.)
Macy's	Department store	109,000
Macy's Men's & Home	Specialty store	67,000
Ralphs Grocery	Supermarket	43,278

Dark and cluttered interiors (left center) at Manhattan Village were replaced by beach-inspired design: water features (top left) and beach furniture in the food area (bottom left).

Soft seating areas add to the "beach house" ambience.

Bare storefronts (above) gave way to canopies and palm trees (right).

The "beach village" look is applied at every opportunity at the renovated mall.

rafters. Inset carpets and over-scaled pots planted with native beach grasses complement new soft seating areas, which are accented by new lighting.

An existing fountain got new life as a tide pool. New interior and exterior landscaping was inspired by beach vegetation that included grasses and palm trees. A new color scheme using a fresh, tone-on-tone palette suggests the subtle color shifts of a sandy beach. Ceramic tile floors were replaced with a sand-colored stone featuring nautilus fossils, thus completing the "beach village"" image.

Phase II capitalized on the "walk-streets" throughout Manhattan Beach and Hermosa Beach. The area is located on a gradual plateau. "Walkstreets" are essentially public sidewalks running between homes, allowing easy access to the nearby beach. Phase II of the mall redevelopment began with replacement of a pad building by an open-air extension for up to four new tenants. The intimate scale, architecture and craftsmanship of the facades and the hardscape detailing and lush landscape of the street lend the "walkstreet" ambience and beach

lifestyle to the mall's new area, which has trellises, shutters and climbing vines.

The mall remained open throughout the construction. Most activity took place at night to reduce the impact on shopper traffic. Despite work at the mall entrances, the mall could not replace the ingress and egress paths, so protected exit passages were built to shield shoppers from construction.

The upscale design and renovation has attracted several new lifestyle tenants, such as Coach, LA Food Show, Corner Bakery and Tommy Bahama. Environmental graphics and identity for the mall were redesigned to echo the mall's new beach image.

Manhattan Village achieved its goal of appealing to South Bay's upscale market while finding new ways to reach out to the community with inviting design.

Prudential Center

Boston, Massachusetts, United States

Owner and Management Company:
Boston Properties
Boston, Massachusetts, United States

Design Architect:
CBT/Childs Bertman Tseckares Inc.
Boston, Massachusetts, United States

Gross size of center:
602,000 sq. ft.

Amount of space renovated:
602,000 sq. ft.

**Gross leasable area
(small shop space, excluding anchors):**
365,000 sq. ft.

Total acreage of site:
23 acres

Type of center:
Regional center

Physical description:
Enclosed mall

Location of trading area:
Regional (suburban and urban)

Population:
- Primary trading area
  61,281

- Secondary trading area
  166,323

- Annualized percentage of shoppers
  anticipated to be from outside trade area
  33%

Development schedule:
- Prudential Tower (office building)
  Original opening date
  1965

- Prudential Center (The Shops)
  Original opening date
  1963

- Current expansion date
  April 2003

Parking spaces:
- Present number
  3,835

The redevelopment of Prudential Center's Huntington Avenue access finally linked the 40-year-old mixed-use project to its neighborhood.

Prudential Center is a landmark in Boston's famed Back Bay – a 3.2-million-square-foot mixed-use urban center containing 602,000 square feet of retail space. This was the second major expansion and renovation of the 40-year-old structure. When built in the 1960s, the complex was oriented to shield itself from derelict surroundings and constructed two stories above street level to span the then-new Massachusetts Turnpike. It was separated from its neighborhood by outdoor plazas, virtually unusable in Boston's long winters.

New owners bought the complex in 1998 and set a goal of repositioning and expanding the center as a premier retail, business, civic and residential address. In addition to the supermarket and 92,000 square feet of retail space, the renovated complex includes a "Class A" office building and a public promenade stretching 480 feet and soaring 50 feet high. An 11-story luxury condominium

Retailers like The Cheesecake Factory saw record sales from the renovation.

MAJOR TENANTS		
NAME	**TYPE**	**GLA (SQ. FT.)**
Lord & Taylor	Department store	124,779
Saks Fifth Avenue	Department store	109,552
Shaw's Supermarket	Supermarket	57,235
Fitcorp Fitness Center	Fitness center	30,916
Barnes & Noble Booksellers	Bookstore	28,500

The Huntington Arcade (below) is 480 feet long and includes Barnes & Noble, Starbucks and retail kiosks.

Fountains and landscaping welcome shoppers to Prudential Center's new arcade (above).

The interior Center Court (top left) was dark. The new court (top right) shows off retailers to greater advantage. Design in the new supermarket building (above) is both practical and attractive.

The supermarket exterior elevations (below) and the view of the South Garden (below right) demonstrate Prudential Center's commitment to beautifying the community.

tower is part of the complex. There is also an open-air park featuring full-sized plantings, movable seating and a built-in stage. The new supermarket is the largest grocery store built in Boston in decades and provides an important amenity to Back Bay and South End residents.

The project required extensive interface with a host of government and public entities, including the Massachusetts Turnpike Authority, the Amtrak national train authority, the Massachusetts Bay Transportation Authority (on subway issues) and the Prudential Project Advisory Committee (PruPAC), an umbrella entity of 22 neighborhood, civic and business groups and public officials.

Perhaps the greatest achievement of the renovation is that Prudential Center finally connects with city streets and neighborhoods. The very protection from decrepit neighborhoods sought in the original design had become its greatest drawback as the area rejuvenated as a desirable residential community. Perimeter service roadways – which separated the center from the city — were

replaced with new retail storefronts and residential and office building entrances at street level.

Renovation of Prudential Center reclaimed an area long dismissed of retail potential. Its Barnes & Noble became one of the top-selling stores in the chain and held the most successful café. The Cheesecake Factory in the center became one of the top five most profitable in the restaurant's 74-unit chain. The center's additional traffic attracted four retail kiosks, adding unanticipated income. Overall, Prudential Center ranked among the top five shopping centers in the United States in 2003, drawing 50,000 visitors a day to the center and providing new gathering places for the community.